Dialogue

A BUSY WRITER'S GUIDE

Marcy Kennedy

Tongue Untied Communications
ONTARIO, CANADA

Marcy Kennedy
marcykennedy@gmail.com
www.marcykennedy.com

Book Layout ©2013 BookDesignTemplates.com
Edited by Christopher Saylor

Dialogue/ Marcy Kennedy. —1st ed.
ISBN 978-0-9920371-2-3

Contents

Why A Busy Writer's Guide?

E very how-to-become-a-better-writer list includes studying craft. Years ago, as a new writer, I took that advice to heart but found that many craft books didn't give me the detailed, in-the-trenches coverage of a topic I needed. They included a lot of beautifully written prose and theory without explaining how to practically apply the principles, or they gave numerous examples but didn't explain how to replicate those concepts in my own work.

I ended up buying three or four books on the same topic to understand it fully and get the balance of theory and practice I was looking for. I spent more time studying craft than writing, and all the exercises in the books seemed to take me away from my story rather than helping me work directly on it. For the modern writer who also needs to blog and be on social media, who might be juggling a day job, and who still wants time to see their family or friends, that's a problem. Do you know anyone who doesn't have more commitments then they're able to handle already without adding "study the writing craft" on top of it?

We're busy. We're tired. We're overworked. We love writing, but often wonder if it's worth the sacrifices we're making for it. We know we're headed down the fast track to burning out, but don't know what we can do differently.

To quote Allan F. Mogensen, the creator of "Work Simplification," it's time to work smarter, not harder.

I wrote *The Busy Writer's Guide* series to help you fast-track the learning process. I felt writers needed a fluff-free guide that would give them the detailed coverage of a topic they required while also respecting their time. I want you to be able to spend the majority of your writing time actually writing, so that you can set aside your computer and enjoy the people and experiences that make life worth living.

Each *Busy Writer's Guide* is intended to serve as an accelerated master's class in a topic. I'll give you enough theory so that you can understand why things work and why they don't, and enough examples to see how that theory looks in practice. I'll also provide tips and exercises to help you take it to the pages of your own story with an editor's-eye view.

My goal is for you to come away a stronger writer, with a stronger piece of work, than when you came in.

CHAPTER ONE

How to Format Your Dialogue

The quickest way to make your work look more professional is to format your dialogue properly. This is the foundation for everything else you'll learn. Once you learn these formatting requirements, you'll do them naturally as you write and won't have to think about them.

ONE SPEAKER PER PARAGRAPH

Every time you have a new speaker, you need a new paragraph, even if the dialogue is only one word long.

Whether you personally like the look of it, this is what readers expect. It makes your dialogue easier to understand because they're able to quickly recognize a change in speaker even before you identify who's talking. It also helps you limit the use of speaker attributions (more on that later).

Wrong:

3

"Ella? Are you here?" Susan asked. Ella popped up from behind the desk, cobwebs in her hair and a dirty cloth dangling from her fingers. "I just need another ten minutes to finish."

Right:

"Ella? Are you here?" Susan asked. Ella popped up from behind the desk, cobwebs in her hair and a dirty cloth dangling from her fingers. "I just need another ten minutes to finish."

CHOOSE THE CORRECT FORM OF PUNCTUATION

Improper punctuation of dialogue is one of the most common mistakes I see in manuscripts I edit and critique.

Use a comma at the end of a segment of dialogue (even a complete sentence) when followed by a tag.

A tag is a word such as *said* or *asked*.

"I hate cinnamon jelly beans," Marcy said.

Use a question mark without a comma for a question.

This applies to exclamation marks too.

"Do you like cinnamon jelly beans?" Marcy asked.

I could have replaced *asked* with *said* here and the punctuation would remain the same.

Extra Tip: Although it might look strange at first, you can use the tag said even if your speaker is asking a question. The question mark alone indicates a question, and

technically we're speaking whether the words come out
as a question, an exclamation, or a shout.

"Do you like cinnamon jelly beans?" Marcy said.

This is an option you have, not a requirement.

**If a tag is dividing a sentence, use a comma at the end
of the first section of dialogue and use a comma after
the tag.**

Follow this rule even if the comma wouldn't normally go
there in the same sentence if it wasn't dialogue.

"I hate cinnamon jelly beans," Marcy said, "because
they burn my tongue."

**Use a period after a tag when the first segment of dia-
logue is a complete sentence.**

"I hate cinnamon jelly beans," Marcy said. "I refuse
to eat them."

Use a dash when dialogue is cut off or interrupted.

Do not add any other punctuation in this case.

"It wasn't my—"
"Enough excuses."

Use an ellipsis for dialogue that fades away.

"I just . . ." She wrapped her arms around her stom-
ach. "I thought he loved me."

Use exclamation marks sparingly!

Sometimes you need an exclamation point to add emotional context, but they're usually a sign that you're trying to bol-

ster weak dialogue. They're also distracting!! And if you use them too often, they lose their emphasis!!

Don't use colons or semicolons in your dialogue at all.

While this might seem like an arbitrary rule, colons and semicolons just look unnatural in dialogue. For the most part, you should avoid them in your fiction entirely. The old joke is that you're allowed one semi-colon per career, so use it wisely.

Punctuation always goes inside the quotation marks in North America.

If you're not in North America, check some of the traditionally published books on your shelf to see where they place punctuation.

USE A TAG OR A BEAT, BUT NOT BOTH

Remember, a tag is a word such as *said* or *asked*. A beat is a piece of action used in place of a tag.

The point of a tag is to let the reader know who's saying what. If you've shown them, through a beat, who's talking, you don't need to also tell them through a tag. It's awkward and wordy to use both.

Wrong:

> "Your dog looks like an alien," my brother said, patting Luna on the head.

Right:

> My brother patted Luna on the head. "Your dog looks like an alien."

Right:

"Your dog looks like an alien," my brother said.

Once in a while you can break this rule for effect, but make sure you're doing it purposefully. What benefit does it give you? You'll be giving up tighter writing, so you need to be sure you're getting something more valuable in return in terms of rhythm or pacing.

AVOID CREATIVITY IN YOUR TAGS

When you have a character hiss, growl, beg, demand, or (insert another descriptor here) a sentence, you're violating the "show, don't tell" principle. It's usually a sign of weak dialogue. If you feel like you need to use a tag other than *said* or *asked* for the reader to understand your meaning, you need to rewrite your dialogue and the beats around it to make it stronger and clearer.

Original:

"Get out," he growled.

Improved:

"She doesn't want you here." John shoved him toward the door hard enough that Eddie lost his balance. "I don't want you here. Come back again, and I'm calling the cops."

Trying to get creative with your tags also comes with other consequences. *Said* and *asked* are nearly invisible to readers. Our minds skip over them. More creative tags aren't, so they can quickly become distracting and annoying.

They're also impossible. Go ahead—try to hiss or growl a sentence.

Another way we violate "show, don't tell" in our tags is when we tack on an adverb, such as *he said angrily* or *she said sadly.*

We're telling the reader what emotion the character is feeling rather than showing them through action. It's cheating.

The exception to both these rules is when you need to give your reader an indication of volume. *Whispered, shouted,* and *yelled* are all appropriate as long as you don't overuse them. So is *she said softly.* Someone can speak softly without necessarily whispering, so, in this case, there isn't a stronger verb to use in place of the adverb.

You can also use a modifier to indicate the way they're saying something if you can't convey it through dialogue.

"I guess I can fix it," she said slowly.

You could try to imply a slowness to her speech through action, but there's no way you can really indicate that she spoke the words slowly other than by writing *she said slowly.*

You can probably come up with examples of best-selling authors who use creative tags or adverbs. But just because they do it doesn't make it right. Their writing would be stronger without them too.

If you insist on dialogue tags other than *said, asked,* or ones denoting volume, if you insist on attaching adverbs to your dialogue tags, it won't necessarily destroy your chances at publication. But don't you want to write the strongest book possible?

DO YOU ALWAYS NEED TO USE A TAG OR A BEAT?

Not every line of dialogue needs a tag or a beat to identify the speaker. If you have only two speakers in a scene, you can leave up to three or four lines unattributed.

> Frank tossed the apple to Mary. "An apple a day and all that."
> "I don't like apples."
> "Everyone likes apples."
> "Not me. They crunch. I don't like fruit that crunches."
> Frank held up a hand. "Give it here, then. No sense letting it go to waste."

Why three or four? Well, three is the number most people can easily keep track of. Once you go beyond that, you risk the reader needing to count backward through the dialogue to figure out who's speaking. (Three is a general rule. Occasionally you can have more, but you need to be very careful that it's not confusing.)

It's best to confine unattributed dialogue to a scene with only two speakers in order to avoid confusion. You can judiciously use it if you have more characters in a scene as long as you use it during a time when two characters are volleying back and forth and the rest are silently watching. More on that later.

Always ask yourself, "If I hadn't written it, would I know who was speaking?"

DON'T OVERUSE CHARACTER NAMES IN DIRECT ADDRESS

Dialogue imitates life, and in life we rarely use people's names when we're talking to them. Yet, when writing dialogue, we often fall into a pattern that looks something like this...

> "Hey, Abby. Was that you I saw at the movie store today?"
> "Why would I go there, Joe? I hate movies."
> "Sorry, Abby. My mistake."

We might be trying to avoid overusing dialogue tags. We might be trying to keep things straight in a scene with multiple characters. But whatever the reason, it sounds artificial and awkward.

Listen to when we address someone by their name in real life. It usually happens in three situations:

1. It's the beginning or end of a conversation, and we're saying hello or goodbye.
2. We're trying to get someone's attention.
3. We're angry or upset and using their name for emphasis, almost as a weapon.

That's when you should use names in your dialogue, and even then, be sparing about it.

Like most writing "rules," we can almost always find an exception—a good way to break it. In this case, you could leverage an overuse of personal names as an element of characterization. A character who is seeking premature intimacy because they're insecure or because they need to gain the other character's confidence (usually to deceive them or sell them something) will tend to overuse names. Go listen to a used car salesman talk and you'll know what I mean.

IDENTIFY THE SPEAKER EARLY

When you have long passages of dialogue, it's usually best to either begin with a beat, so readers know who's talking before they start, or to place a beat or tag at the first natural pause.

Here's an example from my co-written novel, *The Amazon Heir*:

> "We have come to witness our finest warriors compete," Penthesilea said. "Scythia offers their best to us, so we offer them no less. Six stand ready today. We need only three."

If you wait until the end of a long passage like this to clue your reader in to who's speaking, you risk them making an assumption about the speaker and being jarred out of the story when you belatedly tell them their assumption was wrong.

DELETE REDUNDANCY

Redundancy happens when you repeat something in your dialogue that you've already written in either narrative or action.

> He shook his head. "No."

Unless your character needs to add extra emphasis to their denial, the action or the dialogue alone is usually enough.

Let's look at a sneakier example of redundancy.

> Rob glanced at the clock on the wall. Three at last. Time for him to go. He popped his head into Joan's office. "It's three. I'm heading out. Want me to lock up?"

The redundancy here isn't as exact as in the previous example, but it still makes for boring, flabby writing. You could tighten it to read...

> Rob glanced at the clock on the wall. Three at last. He popped his head into Joan's office. "I'm heading out. Want me to lock up?"

Redundancy can also happen big-picture. If, for example, you're going to have a character cracking a safe, you don't need to have them explain the whole process to another character before it happens. That makes it boring for the reader to then have to sit through the description of your character actually cracking the safe (even if something goes wrong).

Repetition is only good if it's intentional and done with a light hand.

HOW LONG SHOULD A CHARACTER BE ALLOWED TO TALK?

As a general rule, don't allow your character to speak more than three sentences in a row without a break. (The rule of three comes in handy a lot in writing.) Follow this guideline even for a character who rambles or who is ranting.

With a ranting or rambling character, interrupt them with another character, even if they have to cut that character off and talk over them.

You can also break up the dialogue with action or internal monologue.

For example, does your rambling/ranting character notice the other character's body-language reactions to what they're saying? Does your rambling/ranting character move around the setting, emphasizing their words with their actions?

If you absolutely must have your character speaking for more than a paragraph, leave off the end quotation mark from the first paragraph and then start the next paragraph with another beginning quotation mark. Close the second paragraph with an end quotation mark.

TAKE IT TO THE PAGE

If you're working on your first draft, or if you're reading this book to get a working knowledge of the topic but aren't ready yet to work on revising/editing your book based on what you're learning, skip the "Take It to the Page" section at the end of each chapter. When you're ready to start rewrites/edits, you can always come back to them.

For those of you who are ready to start rewrites or edits, you have two options for how you apply the exercises for this chapter.

Option A – This method takes longer, but is more thorough. Using either the highlighter tool in your word processing program or a green highlighter and a paper printout, highlight all your dialogue (only what's between the quotation marks—don't highlight tags or beats). For this particular chapter, it'll be easier if you use the highlighter tool in your word processing program. Follow the Option A path below.

Option B – This method is quicker, but less thorough. You'll still need to pay attention during your final round of edits to make sure you haven't missed anything (or trust that the freelance editor you hire or the editor at your publisher will catch whatever you miss), but this path allows you to do triage and move on to the next chapter. No highlighting for you. You'll be using both the Find and Replace feature of your word processing program and your memory of your story. Follow the Option B path below.

Option A Path

Now that your highlights show you where your dialogue is without you having to read every word you've written, you're ready to go. I've tried to minimize the number of times you'll need to go through your work, but there's really no way of getting around multiple passes if you want to do a thorough job.

I recommend you follow the steps for one chapter at a time rather than trying to work Step 1 through the entire story and then coming back to the start for Step 2. Going chapter by chapter is quicker. Once you finish, don't throw away your pages or remove your green highlighting. You'll be using it again later.

Step 1 – Either lay your pages out on the table or zoom out in your computer file. Do you have large chunks of uninterrupted green? (This is why I had you only highlight what came between the quotation marks and not the tags and beats.) Use the suggestions in this chapter to break up those chunks. If you're still having trouble with how to do this, save this step until after Chapter Two, where we'll talk more about adding variety to dialogue.

Step 2 – For every highlighted passage of dialogue at a time, check for the following punctuation problems:
- ✓ Have you used the correct punctuation (comma/period/question mark)?
- ✓ Does your dialogue include an exclamation mark? Read each passage of dialogue with an exclamation mark out loud to see if you actually would (and can) exclaim the passage. Does the sentence need it to

make the meaning clear? Can you rewrite the sentence to make it more powerful so that it doesn't need the exclamation mark?

✓ Does your dialogue include a semicolon? Change it to a period.

Step 3 – For every highlighted passage of dialogue at a time, check for the following tag and beat issues:

✓ Do you have a single speaker per paragraph?

✓ If you have multiple lines of unattributed dialogue (that is, dialogue without a tag or a beat), is it clear who's speaking?

✓ For longer passages of dialogue, have you either preceded them with a beat or identified the speaker using a tag at the first natural pause?

✓ Have you used a tag and a beat together? If so, delete the tag. You don't need it.

✓ Is your tag *said*, *asked*, *whispered*, or *yelled*? If so, good. If not, replace your more creative tag with one of these.

✓ Does your dialogue tag have an adverb attached to it? Does the adverb indicate something you couldn't convey through either a stronger verb or stronger dialogue? If not, rewrite your dialogue and beats so that you can delete the adverb.

Step 4 – Now it's time to read each passage of highlighted dialogue, along with the tags and beats belonging to it.

✓ Do you have one character addressing another by name in their dialogue? Ninety-nine percent of the time, you should delete the direct address.

✓ Do you have redundancy between your dialogue and the beats around it?

Option B Path

Open the Find box in whatever word-processing program you use. It's about to become your best friend.

Step 1 – Search for the following. The first two examples have no space between the punctuation and the quotation mark. Make sure to include a space between the punctuation and the quotation marks in the second two examples.

"
'

."

,"
'

."

(In case you find that difficult to read, it's comma-quotation mark, period-quotation mark, comma-space-quotation mark, and period-space-quotation mark.)

Check that you've used them correctly. This won't catch everything, but it will clean up your dialogue punctuation significantly.

Step 2 – Search for exclamation marks. Read each passage of dialogue with an exclamation mark out loud to see if you actually would (and can) exclaim the passage. Does the sentence need it to make the meaning clear? Can you rewrite the sentence to make it more powerful so that it doesn't need the exclamation mark?

Step 3 – Search for semicolons. Replace them with periods.

Step 4 – Run a search for the words in the following list. Are you telling rather than showing? Do you absolutely need these words to get your meaning across, or is there another way you could show the meaning? Rewrite so that you only need to use *said, asked, whispered, yelled,* or the adverb examples discussed in this chapter.

acknowledged
admitted
agreed
angled
answered
argued
babbled
barked
begged
bellowed
bemoaned
blurted
blustered
bragged
breathed
commented
complained
confessed
cried
croaked
crooned
crowed
demanded
denied
drawled

echoed

faltered

fumed

giggled

groaned

growled

grumbled

heckled

hinted

hissed

howled

implored

inquired

inserted

interjected

interrupted

jested

laughed

mumbled

murmured

muttered

nagged

offered

opined

orated

pleaded

pouted

promised

queried

questioned

quipped

quoted
raged
ranted
reiterated
remembered
replied
requested
retorted
roared
ruminated
sang
scolded
screamed
screeched
shouted
shrieked
sighed
snarled
snickered
snorted
sobbed
sputtered
stammered
stuttered
threatened
thundered
told
wailed
warned
whimpered
whined

wondered

yelped

Step 5 – Search for the words asked and said. Each time you find one, ask yourself these questions.

- ✓ Have I used both a tag and a beat? If so, remove the tag. Your writing will immediately be tighter.
- ✓ Do I have only one speaker in this paragraph? If you have more than one speaker, create separate paragraphs.
- ✓ Have I used a tag or a beat early enough to identify the speaker for long passages of dialogue?
- ✓ Does this passage of dialogue run for more than three or four sentences? If it does, how could you break it up?

If you'd like a printable version of the complete revision checklist (material from all the chapters) for your Option Path and links to other helpful posts on dialogue, go to www.marcykennedy.com/dialogue and use the password below.

Password: saywhat

CHAPTER TWO

Adding Variety to Your Dialogue

Very rarely is good dialogue a simple, back-and-forth, on-the-nose exchange. While there are times for that in your life and fiction, if you default to it too often, your dialogue starts to sound bland and unnatural. You end up with a bored reader and can't figure out why. You ask yourself "Isn't dialogue active by nature?" (It's not.)

The way to avoid this problem is to give the illusion of listening to real speech by imitating real speech patterns.

ANSWER WITH A QUESTION

When someone asks you a question you'd rather not answer, how do you react? Often people deflect with another question.

> "I tried calling you last night. Where were you?"
> "Where do you think I was?"

We can use this when we have a character with a guilty conscience, but the deflection doesn't have to be due to something the character has done wrong. Sometimes we might want to use a question in answer as a way to tease another person. Sometimes we don't feel like answering a question because it feels like someone is prying into private matters.

For example, in Part 3, Chapter 2 of Fyodor Dostoyevsky's *Crime and Punishment*, Razumikhin is a good man who doesn't like it when the doctor who's caring for his sick friend starts asking questions about the family's financial situation and criticizing the choice Razumikhin's friend made to turn away an unworthy but wealthy suitor for his sister. The doctor speaks first in this example...

> "Why is he so set against this Luzhin? A man with money and she doesn't seem to dislike him... and they haven't a farthing, I suppose? Eh?"
> "But what business is it of yours?" Razumihin cried with annoyance. "How can I tell whether they've a farthing?"

Dostoyevsky could have written this exchange as...

> "Why is he so set against this Luzhin? A man with money and she doesn't seem to dislike him...and they haven't a farthing, I suppose? Eh?"
> "I don't know if they have any money, and it's none of our business either way."

It would have served the same purpose, but been much less interesting and less powerful.

INTERRUPT

Interruption can characterize a person who's impatient or self-centered by nature (we'll talk more about using dialogue for characterization in a later chapter). It can heat up an argument or give the reader insight into a deteriorating relationship. It can also indicate a character who's fed up with the badgering of another character.

> "You really need to—"
> "I know. You don't need to keep reminding me."

You can also use this to mimic the way we tend to talk over each other or interrupt in real life because we don't want to hear what the other person has to say, we want to correct something they've said that's wrong, or we're so excited to say our piece that we don't wait for the other person to finish. Interruption can be used equally well with two joking characters as it can with two fighting characters.

New York Times bestselling romance author Jude Deveraux employs this tactic liberally (perhaps a little too liberally at times). If you want to see this in action, take a look at the first chapter of Deveraux's *High Tide* using the preview feature offered by online retailers.

ECHO

In real life, we often echo a word when we're nervous, lying, or stalling for time.

> "Do you think she's pretty?"
> "Pretty?"

It can also be a sign of someone who's confused and is trying to wrap their mind around what you've just said, or of someone who is trying to fully understand what was just said.

It's also a common tactic used by children trying to annoy someone else.

MISDIRECTION/NON-RESPONSE

And sometimes, if the conversation isn't going where we want it to, we just refuse to go along with it.

> "We're going to lose our reservation. You almost ready to go?"
> "I saw you with her again today."

It's also a great delay tactic. In Lindsay Buroker's steampunk novella *Flash Gold*, Kali McAlister is alone in her workshop when a large man enters. She uses misdirection and non-response to keep from telling him her name until she can reach a weapon to defend herself, just in case he turns out to want to harm her. (Something she has reason to fear given her history.)

> "You Kali McAlister?" he asked, voice smoother and more pleasant than his rough exterior hinted at.
> "Ma'am." She propped her hands on her hips by way of disguising another step toward the lever. "It's polite to call a lady 'ma'am.' Even if she's a half-breed wearing a man's trousers with tools sticking out of all her pockets." Not to mention she was only eighteen and covered in grease. She would collapse in surprise if anyone called her ma'am without the ulterior motive of needing a favor.
> He stared at her for a long moment. "You Kali McAlister? Ma'am."
> "I reckon that depends on who you are." She pretended to scratch her knee and took another step.
> "Your identity changes depending on your caller?"
> "Sometimes it does." Another step.
> "Cedar."
> "What?"
> "My name."
> "That's not a name," she said. "That's a tree."

Kali could have answered him directly and lunged for the lever to release her weapon, but by using dialogue this way, Buroker stretches the suspense and also gives us insight into Kali's personality and verbal abilities. Buroker's strength is dialogue, so if you want to study someone who does it well, pick up a few of her books.

LET SILENCE SPEAK

In Ernest Hemingway's classic short story "Hills Like White Elephants," a man is trying to convince his girlfriend to get an abortion. Her reaction—silence. And it conveys her resistance to his suggestion more clearly than if she'd said it aloud.

> "It's really an awfully simple operation, Jig," the man said. "It's not really an operation at all."
> The girl looked at the ground the table legs rested on.
> "I know you wouldn't mind it, Jig. It's really not anything. It's just to let the air in."

Your character might resort to silence for a number of reasons. Maybe they're passive-aggressive, maybe they're afraid of angering the person they're talking to, or maybe they feel like nothing they could say would make a difference anyway.

ADD SUBTEXT

In *Creating Unforgettable Characters*, author and Hollywood script director Linda Seger describes subtext as "what the character is really saying beneath and between the lines." It's when characters talk around a subject, but still know what's going on.

In the episode "Trial and Error" of the old TV show *Joan of Arcadia*, Joan (a high school student) takes part in a mock trial where she's prosecuting Jack from *Jack and the Beanstalk* for stealing the giant's golden goose. Her boyfriend, Adam, plays Jack. Just before Joan examines Adam on the stand, she accidentally finds out Adam cheated on her.

Joan is angry and hurt, but she doesn't know how to confront Adam. Instead, she channels everything she's feeling into her questioning of Jack about why he stole the giant's goose. Did he need the goose or did he only want it? Wasn't it true he'd already had a full meal and so he didn't need the goose? Do you believe that just because you want something, it's okay to take it no matter what the consequences are?

Joan and Adam are having one conversation while those watching the trial are hearing something else.

(As of the writing of this edition, you can watch this clip on You Tube by searching for "Joan of Arcadia Trial Part 1." Watch the different reactions of the teenagers playing Jack's defense attorneys. The girl is Joan's best friend and realizes what's going on. The boy is Joan's brother and has no idea what's happening.)

Subtext is that argument with your husband about not replacing the empty toilet paper roll that isn't about toilet paper at all, but rather about how you feel like he doesn't help you out, doesn't think about you at all.

It's the conversation with your girlfriend where she wants to go to the same restaurant you always go to and you want to try something new, which is actually about how she's happy with your relationship the way it is but you want some adventure.

It's the threat from the woman whose job you took veiled in a jab about a dead plant.

Try using subtext in an emotionally charged conversation that would otherwise be in danger of melodrama if you wrote it directly. You'll also often find subtext in a conversation where characters can't speak openly for fear of being overheard or when one character isn't brave enough to openly talk to another character about what's on their mind.

USE HUMOR

Human beings like to laugh, and so our conversations are filled with good-natured teasing, jokes, double entendres, and tongue-in-cheek quips. Authentic dialogue will sometimes include the same things, even in the most serious story.

Match humor to your characters' personalities.

Not everyone can shoot off amazing one-liners (I can't). Is your character the type to use sarcasm? Or does she have a dry sense of humor? Perhaps he likes corny jokes and puns.

If you give all your characters the same type of humor, a type that doesn't fit their personality, it's going to feel forced. And forced humor is never funny.

Surprise the reader/listener.

This should make sense. The joke you laughed hysterically at the first time isn't funny the fifth time you hear it. Freshness, the surprise, was what elevated it to funny. If you want your dialogue to be truly funny, you need to also look for a fresh way to write things. This might mean re-writing a line of dialogue multiple times to get it right.

Avoid being too painful or offensive.

Have you ever noticed that some comedians are masters at walking the line between funny and offensive, while other comedians anger half the audience? This is a much more difficult skill to master than surprise. When you poke fun, it needs to be done tastefully so that people can laugh at themselves. It's all too easy to go too far so that the joke becomes mean. One of the reasons *The Simpsons* has run for so many years is the writers know how to walk this line.

You also need to take care that the subject matter of your joke is tasteful. No one wants to hear a joke about rape or child abuse.

Study the masters.

Dissect the work of an author you think is funny, and take notes on what they did and exactly how they did it. Watch videos of comedians on YouTube.

Know your audience.

I'll often roll my eyes or be disgusted by the things my husband (a former Marine) finds hilarious. The reverse is true. What makes me laugh so hard I snort barely merits an eye roll from him. Humor is subjective. Know your target audience and what they find funny.

Humorous dialogue will come more naturally to some writers than to others. If you can't write humor, don't worry about it. You have other strengths that a funny writer may not have.

But don't give up on writing humor too quickly, either. Because this book isn't about humor writing, I couldn't spend too much time on it, but I've collected links to other resources for you. Make sure you use the password at the end of this book to gain access to the supplementary resources on my website.

CAN WE GO TOO FAR IN IMITATING REAL SPEECH PATTERNS?

The advice to imitate real speech patterns can definitely go too far. Real speech is often boring to listen to if you're not part of the conversation. (Sometimes it's even boring to listen to if you are.)

Cut out the "filler" of *ums*, *ers*, and *ahs*.

Even though we regularly use these in our speech, they don't add anything to dialogue.

Skip all the chit-chat and social niceties.

We don't need to hear the character say hello, ask each other how they've been, and all the other small talk we make on a daily basis because it's the polite thing to do. Those don't forward the story, and, as we'll see in the next chapter, all dialogue needs a strong reason to exist. In dialogue, go straight to the important stuff and cut the fluff.

TAKE IT TO THE PAGE

If you've forgotten whether you're an Option A or an Option B person, go back to Chapter One and find out.

Option A Path

Look at the green-highlighted segments in each chapter and follow the steps below.

Step 1 – Do any of your highlighted segments include "filler" like *um*s, *er*s, and *ah*s? Cut them and find a way to show your character's hesitation through action beats instead.

Step 2 – Have you indulged in throat-clearing? This is where you include hellos and goodbyes, characters talking about the weather (without there being some subtext to the conversation), or characters asking, "How are you?" Try cutting those sections. Did you really need them for the scene to work? Or had you put them there trying to imitate real life? Most of the time you should be able to cut them and the scene will be immediately stronger.

Step 3 – Have you been too straightforward in a conversation? Try adding an answer with a question, an interruption, an echo, or a misdirection/non-response. Did it increase the tension and conflict?

Step 4 – Does the chapter include emotionally charged dialogue? Is it bordering on melodrama because you've approached it directly? Try re-writing using silence, subtext, or a combination of both.

Step 5 – Would it be appropriate for your characters to tease each other? Could you add humor to offset the tension in a scene (this is another way to avoid melodrama)? Could a touch of humor transform a situation that might otherwise feel clichéd because we've seen it so many times (e.g., a first kiss, a job interview)?

Step 6 – Read a page or two of your dialogue out loud. (You can skip everything in between. You only need to hear the dialogue itself.) Does it sound natural or stilted? If it sounds too formal, that's a sign you're probably writing in too many complete sentences. Go through all of your dialogue and see if you can loosen it up through sentence fragments and less-perfect grammar.

Option B Path

Step 1 – Use the Find feature to run a search for *um*s, *er*s, and *ah*s (use the spelling you would have used for each). Delete them. If you still feel you need something to show hesitation in your character, rewrite the action beats around your dialogue.

Step 2 – Use the Find feature to run a search for *hello* and *goodbye*. These can be signs of throat-clearing. This is where you "warm up" before the conflict or "wind down" rather than ending the scene on a strong line. Try cutting those sections. Did you really need them for the scene to work? Or had you put them there trying to imitate real life? Most of the time you should be able to cut them and the scene will be immediately stronger.

Step 3 – Use the Find feature to search for *How are you?* or any variation you might personally use. This phrase can also be an indicator of boring dialogue or the throat-clearing we searched for in Step 2. Follow the same process of seeing how much you can cut.

Step 4 – Make a list of the five most emotionally charged scenes in your novel. Check each of them. Are they bordering on melodrama because you've approached them directly? Try re-writing them using silence, subtext, or a combination of both.

Step 5 – Think about your story and try to identify each of the following:
- ✓ A scene when you have a character who doesn't want to tell the truth to the person they're talking to. Can you add an echo, or answer with a question?
- ✓ A scene when you have an impatient character, or where you want to show a relationship starting to disintegrate. Can you add an interruption?
- ✓ A scene where someone needs to stall for time. Can you add an echo?
- ✓ A scene where someone is tired of another character refusing to address the real issue. Can you add a non-response to a question?

✓ A scene where two characters disagree about what to do next. Have you written it as an argument? Would it become more powerful if you used silence instead to show one character's resistance?

✓ A scene that's borderline melodramatic. Can you add some humor to offset the highly charged emotions in the scene and bring it back from the melodrama cliff?

✓ A scene where you want to show relationship growth between characters. Would some lighthearted teasing or banter be appropriate?

Step 6 – Read a page or two of your dialogue out loud. (You can skip everything in between. You only need to hear the dialogue itself.) Does it sound natural or stilted? If it sounds too formal, that's a sign you're probably writing in too many complete sentences. Go through all of your dialogue and see if you can loosen it up through sentence fragments and less-perfect grammar.

CHAPTER THREE

Does Your Dialogue Deserve to Exist?

The biggest mistake writers make when it comes to dialogue isn't what you might expect.

The biggest mistake we make is forgetting that dialogue—like everything else in fiction—needs a reason to exist.

If dialogue comes easily to you, then this is going to be something you need to watch. Because dialogue is your strength, your tendency will be to allow your dialogue to dominate your story, which isn't necessarily a bad thing, but it can also trip you up. You'll be prone to adding empty small talk or to depending on dialogue to the exclusion of other action, internal dialogue, and description. A well-rounded story needs them all.

To give your dialogue a reason to exist, make sure every passage does at least one of these three things. (Bonus points if it does more than one.)

REVEAL CHARACTER OR CHARACTER RELATIONSHIPS

In my short story "A Purple Elephant" (in my ebook *Frozen*), I knew I didn't have much space to flesh out the relationship between my point-of-view character and her husband. (Short stories are a great training ground for learning to do a lot with a little.) I wanted to open with a passage that showed something about their relationship, as well as introduced my main character (the narrator).

> I found my goldfish in my freezer in a plastic baggie, the kind I use to pack my husband macadamia nut cookies in his lunch. I don't remember tucking her in the baggie. I don't remember putting her in the freezer. I don't remember killing her.
>
> But I must have. For ten minutes, I stared at her lying on top of a bag of peas, gold against green, the freezer door hanging open, and tried to think of any other way she could have ended up there. None came to mind.
>
> I closed the door and called my husband on his cell phone. Because he manages all five of the restaurants that I inherited from my father, I could never know which he'd be at. He might be ten minutes from me or two hours.
>
> He picked up on the second ring. "Gerry Lawrence."
>
> "I think I'm doing it again."
>
> "Candice?"
>
> "I think I'm doing it again."
>
> "Do you want me to come home?"
>
> "I think I'm doing it again."
>
> "I'll be there in twenty minutes."

By the time we've finished these seven lines of dialogue, we know Candice is unbalanced and depends heavily on her husband. We know he doesn't think she's pulling a prank and he doesn't need to ask what she's doing—whatever is going on, it's a pattern for them and they have enough trust in their relationship that, when she calls, he comes.

For an excellent example of this, I also recommend reading Janice Hardy's *The Shifter*, a middle-grade fantasy. Early in the book, Hardy needs to introduce twin boys and set them apart (always a challenge with characters who are twins). She does this in a few ways, including introducing us to one individually before bringing them together and describing their body language. But the main tool she uses is their dialogue. It reveals many layers of information about the characters and their relationships. You know that Jovan is naturally braver and more selfless than Bahari. Jovan's also a leader, and Bahari will eventually do as he's told.

I'll go into detail in a later chapter about how a character's personality affects their speech patterns.

Dialogue can also be used to reveal a character's priorities and past.

A character who talks about their family all the time (in a positive way) is demonstrating how important their family is to them.

A character who claims their family is important but spends all their time on their own hobbies and activities is showing the reader they're a hypocrite. You never have to tell your reader that if you show it to them by contrasting their words with their actions.

You can also use speech as a natural way to weave in snippets of backstory or to give your reader a hint about what your character dreams about and desires most.

In addition, the way we speak to someone reveals our relationship to them.

Whenever your character speaks to someone else, their dialogue should be tailored to who they're speaking to. If you can swap the listener without changing the dialogue, you need to rethink how you're writing it.

How close are the characters?

Are they comfortable enough with each other to tease? To disagree? To point out the seed stuck between the other person's teeth?

Do they have a history that colors everything they say to each other? Have their past interactions been good or bad?

Will this conversation take their relationship to a new level of closeness? Will it destroy the closeness they have?

What's the hierarchy?

Is the speaker talking to a superior, an equal, or an inferior?

The way we give a suggestion to our boss is very different from the way we give a suggestion to our spouse, which is also very different from the way we give a suggestion to our teenager.

The way a nurse talks to a patient is different from the way she talks to a doctor, which is different from the way she talks to her accountant.

Hierarchy is subjective as well as objective. For example, a new owner might be objectively higher on the office totem pole than his factory foreman. However, if the foreman is the one who knows the business best and has the trust of the workers, the owner might be subjectively higher in certain conversations where the owner has to defer to his opinion or suffer the consequences.

What role is each character trying to play?

Is this a cooperative conversation where they're trying to solve a problem together as teammates?

Is this a power struggle where one character is trying to control the other and take the role of leader?

Is this a case of a weaker character trying to ingratiate themselves with a stronger character so they have a protector?

Is this a situation where one rational character is trying to reason with a character they see as irrational?

Is someone lying?

Is there a romantic involvement? What type?

People who are newly dating speak to each other differently than a couple who's been married for five years does. A newly dating couple will be more tentative, wanting to put their best foot forward. A couple who's been married five years will have private jokes, old wounds, and a closeness that allows them to convey their meaning without explicitly stating it if the marriage is good. How a couple speaks to each other reveals a lot about the condition of their marriage.

ADVANCE THE PLOT

We hear the advice to "show, don't tell" so often it's almost clichéd.

Using dialogue to advance the plot makes our scenes more active, avoids author intrusion, and "shows."

But what does it mean to say dialogue is advancing the plot? Dialogue can advance the plot by…

- providing new information
- increasing suspense, tension, or conflict through an argument, a threat, confusion, etc.
- revealing new obstacles
- reminding us of the characters' scene or story goals

If you cut the dialogue, does the scene still make sense? If so, it doesn't advance the plot.

Can your character say something that makes the reader worry about the outcome of what's about to happen? Can they cast doubt on whether their plan will succeed?

Does she receive information that brings her a step closer to her goal? Does he learn something that sets him back?

Does it remind the reader of your character's goal and why they want it?

Do the words of another character make them regret their actions? Strengthen their resolve?

Does it bring to light something that, after they've achieved their goal, changes the way they see and understand what just happened?

Michael Crichton was a master at conveying through dialogue information that could be dry or boring and doing it in such a way that it feels natural and keeps you turning pages. Even if you don't want to read *Jurassic Park* from cover to cover, I recommend you read the chapter titled "The Park," paying close attention to the part where Dr. Alan Grant and the two children are stranded in the park with a *Tyrannosaurus* after them and no way to call for help. They're trying to get back to the visitor center, where they think they'll be safe, and they need to get back quickly because they have to stop the boat that recently left the island before it reaches the mainland. The boat captain doesn't realize three juvenile velociraptors stowed away on the ship.

The quickest way back seems to be to take a raft down the river. The three of them sneak past the sleeping *T. Rex*, and Dr. Grant paddles them out into the middle of the lagoon.

This would be the point where most readers would breathe a sigh of relief, thinking the tension would finally let up. Crichton needs a way to tell you they're not safe despite being on the water because tyrannosaurs can swim.

He could have simply written...

> Because tyrannosaurs could swim, they wouldn't be
> safe until they were out of sight.

He could have given us a flat piece of dialogue like this...

> "Stay down and quiet," Grant whispered. "He can
> swim, and he'll follow us out here if he wakes up."

What he does instead is brilliant and does some heavy lifting. (I wish I could share it with you here, but due to copyright issues, I'm unable to quote it. Be sure to check it out!) It increases tension and reveals a new obstacle. The fact that the *T. Rex* can swim is a crucial piece of plot information because it sets up a chase scene down the river that covers approximately the next thirty-five pages. Beyond that, it adds a touch a humor to a horrible situation, reveals character relationships, and continues to characterize Lex.

Throughout the book, Lex almost falls into the too-stupid-to-live category. Even taking into account the fact that she's a young child, she's spoiled and lacks common sense in situations where most children would exhibit it. When you read the passage, make sure to watch for all these things happening seamlessly.

ECHO THE THEME

Every good movie does this. According to Blake Snyder in *Save the Cat*, creating a line of dialogue to echo the theme isn't negotiable—a movie must include it to work.

Good books will do it multiple times in subtle ways.

After Peter Parker forgets to pick up his Aunt May in *The Amazing Spider-Man* and she has to walk home alone at night, putting herself in danger, Uncle Ben is fed up with Peter acting out and shirking responsibility. He tells Peter that his father lived by the code that you're morally obligated to do good things for people if you can.

In other words, when you have a particular talent or ability that could help others, your responsibility as a decent human being is to use your skills to benefit others.

It's a clunky replacement for the traditional Spider-Man theme of *With great power comes great responsibility*. And while on the surface it could seem both the new version and the old version are essentially saying the same thing, Uncle Ben's new line better reflects the subtle questions raised by the plot.

Because in saying that, when we are able to do good things for other people we're morally obligated to do those things, we have to ask ourselves two questions.

Whose definition of *good* are we using?

And do we have a full enough view of the big picture to know what the truly good thing to do would be?

Dr. Connors, the villain in *The Amazing Spider-Man*, wants to release a gas into the air above New York to mutate everyone into giant lizards. As a lizard-person, he's stronger, faster, and able to regenerate. In his own way, Connors believes he'd be helping turn people into something "better." Humanity, in its current state, is weak. He has the power to perfect humanity. Wouldn't that be a *good* thing that's within his ability to do?

And when Peter Parker should have acted to stop the thief who later shot Uncle Ben, he stood by because he felt like the store clerk was getting what he deserved for being a jerk. In some ways, Captain Stacy was right in calling Spider-Man a vigilante. Peter felt that his personal view of justice was the only right one.

For most of the movie, however, Peter's actions fall more cleanly into a category of good accepted by the majority of people. He's catching bad guys and helping advance science. And yet, he acts without a broad enough understanding of the consequences of his actions and the wider implications.

When he goes to dinner at Gwen Stacy's home, he and Captain Stacy argue over whether Spider-Man is a hero or a hooligan. Peter suggests Spider-Man is doing good because he's catching car thieves and other criminals.

Captain Stacy tells him that those criminals are still on the streets because the police want them there—they're bait to catch the men in charge of the crime rings.

The police were working with a bigger understanding. They wanted to catch the person in charge of the car theft ring, not just the low-level, easily replaced lackey Spidey webs to the wall. Were Spidey's actions good? Yes. He took a criminal off the street. But did they also potentially sabotage a greater good and a longer-term plan?

Peter also gives the equation to Dr. Connors that allows the re-growth of limbs but also creates monsters. He didn't know enough about Connor's character or the morality (or lack thereof) of the bigwigs in Oscorp to so blithely share the equation his father worked so hard to hide.

That single line early in the movie is the thematic question that drives the rest of the story.

In Chapter 7 of *The Hunger Games*, Peeta and Katniss argue about which of them has the better chance of survival and of getting sponsors. Each believes it's the other. In exasperation, Peeta turns to Haymitch (their mentor) and tells him that Katniss has no idea of the effect she can have on people.

That we can sometimes make a difference in others' lives without even knowing it is a theme that runs through the entire *Hunger Games* series.

Katniss didn't set out to change the world. She just did what was right and change followed. She had no idea of the chain of events her seemingly small actions would cause.

And Suzanne Collins sums it all up in two sentence fragments.

Echoing the theme doesn't have to be obvious. You can work your theme into dialogue using subtext and foreshadowing as well.

TAKE IT TO THE PAGE

You should be familiar with your Option Path by now. If you're not feeling comfortable with the one you chose, remember that you're not locked in to it. You can switch any time you want (or use a combination of the two).

Option A Path

Step 1 – Mark each passage of green highlighted dialogue with letters for why it deserves to exist: C for character/character relationships, P for plot, and T for theme.

Step 2 – For any passages that weren't marked with a C, could it be? (Remember, the best passages of dialogue will have more than one reason to exist.) Jot down the answers to these questions about the characters who speak to each other in the scene.

✓ What's the hierarchy? Does this come through in how the characters talk to each other?

✓ What role is each character trying to play in the scene?

✓ Are they comfortable enough to disagree, or do they feel like they have to put their best foot forward by always playing nice, even if they don't actually agree? (You can show the difference between their speech and their real opinion using internal dialogue in your point-of-view character.)

✓ What one event in their history together colors their current conversation? Can you use that event to layer added meaning into their conversation?

✓ How will this conversation make their relationship more intimate? Or how will this conversation destroy the closeness they have?

✓ What's one thing that's important to your character? Can you find a place to show this in her dialogue?

✓ Find a character that you want to indicate is unreliable or hypocritical. Is there a way you can contrast what they say with what they do?

Step 3 – For any passage that didn't receive a letter, could you add a P to it by doing one of the following things?

✓ Keeping in mind their goal from the previous scene or their goal for this scene, can you bring to light something that changes the way they see and understand their goal?

✓ Can your character say something that makes the reader worry about the outcome of what's about to happen? Can they cast doubt on whether their plan will succeed?

✓ Does your character learn something that sets him back? Do the words of another character make her regret the action she just performed?

✓ Can she receive information that brings her a step closer to her goal? Can the words of another character help strengthen her resolve?

Step 4 – If you didn't find any places where you could mark a T, spend time figuring out the theme of your novel.

You should have one. Find three places where you can sub-tly express it through your dialogue (if you haven't already).

Option B Path

Step 1 – Skim your book quickly. By *skim* I literally mean *glance at each page*. Don't get bogged down by reading it all through. All you want to do is remind yourself of the dialogue happening in each scene. Ask yourself what purpose each passage serves. If you can legitimately say the passage serves a purpose, move on to the next.

Step 2 – When you hit a passage that doesn't serve a purpose, you need to delete it or rewrite it. If you find your-self unsure of how to make the dialogue serve a purpose, think about these questions.

- ✓ What's one thing that's important to your character? Can you find a place to show this in her dialogue?
- ✓ Does the scene include an unreliable character? Can you use dialogue to contrast what she says with what she's actually doing?
- ✓ Can your character say something that makes the reader worry about the outcome of what's about to happen? Can they cast doubt on whether their plan will succeed?
- ✓ Pick two of the characters who talk to each other in this scene. Can you write a conversation that will make their relationship more intimate? Or one that will destroy the closeness they have?
- ✓ Pick two of the characters who talk to each other in this scene. What one event in their history together colors their current conversation? Can you use that

event to layer added meaning into their conversation?

✓ Can you show a difference between what a character is saying and what they're thinking by using internal monologue (also known as internal dialogue)?

✓ What role is each character trying to play in the scene?

✓ Can your character receive information that brings her a step closer to her goal? Or moves her a step farther away from it?

✓ Can another character say something that makes your hero regret his previous actions?

Step 3 – What's the theme of your novel? Find one additional place where you can subtly express it through dialogue.

CHAPTER FOUR

Conveying Information Through Dialogue

Dialogue is a great way to convey information, but only if you do it right. One question that inevitably comes up after talking about the need for dialogue to have a purpose is the dreaded info dump in dialogue.

In *Revision & Self-Editing*, James Scott Bell says the key to avoiding info dump dialogue is to remember that dialogue is always from one character to another. It can't sound like you're manipulating it (even though you are). It must always be what a character would naturally say.

So even though dialogue needs to serve a purpose to exist, it also still needs to be written for the character's benefit, not for the reader's benefit.

Let me explain that a bit more.

Dialogue written for the reader's benefit feels unnatural because you have characters say things they wouldn't normally say or say them in a way that they wouldn't (often using much more detail than any of us include when we talk).

Dialogue written for the characters fits the context, and is always from one character to another rather than from one character to the reader. It takes more work to achieve, but the result will be worth the effort.

Here are some of the major info dump situations to avoid and how to fix them.

AS-YOU-KNOW-BOB SYNDROME

As the name suggests, As-You-Know-Bob Syndrome is when one character tells another character something they already know. It's done purely for the reader's benefit, and it's unnatural.

A character won't say something the character they're talking to already knows.

For example, a husband won't say to his wife, "When we bought this house two years ago, we emptied our savings for a down payment. We don't have anything left."

The wife already knows when the house was purchased. She knows they emptied their savings. She also knows they haven't been able to replace those savings yet.

Thus, her husband has no reason to say any of that.

Info dumps won't always be this obvious, but if you could add "as you know" to the front of whatever's being said, it's time to rewrite.

If it's common knowledge, it won't come up in conversation.

Let's say you have two sisters meeting to go out for lunch. One shows up at the other's door.

> "Come on in, Susie. I'm just cleaning up the muddy
> paw prints left by our pit bull Jasper."

It's common knowledge her sister owns a pit bull named Jasper. Her sister wouldn't feel the need to state it. She'd be more likely to say...

> "Come in for a sec. I just have to clean up the mud
> the stupid dog tracked in again."

Even essential information needs to be given in a natural way. So if knowing that their dog is a pit bull named Jasper is essential to the story, you could write...

> A flash of fur tore across Ellen's freshly washed floor and threw itself at Susie.
> Susie shoved the dog down. "Off, Jasper."
> He dropped onto his back for a belly rub, tongue lolling out of his mouth.
> Ellen sighed. "Sorry about that. Did he get you dirty?"
> Susie shook her head and scratched Jasper behind the ear. Even if he had, a little mud never hurt anyone. "Any more trouble with the anti-pit bull crowd at the park? Brent said someone threatened to call the cops last week."

A character won't say something that isn't relevant to the conversation.

> "A hundred years ago, when the dam was construct-
> ed, this town was built on the dried-out flood plain. If
> the dam breaks, it'll wipe out the whole place."

Did you catch the sneaky insertion of backstory in adding "a hundred years ago"? What normal person would actually say that? Who would care how long ago the dam was built when the real issue is whether or not the town is about to be destroyed?

If we have two town residents talking, they also know the town is built on a flood plain. While that's relevant to the conversation, it violates the common knowledge rule. Find a more creative way to bring in the information.

How can we avoid As-You-Know-Bob Syndrome?

Figure out what information is essential to the scene and only include that.

Let's look at an example where two brothers are being held captive. Their kidnapper leaves them locked in a room during the day while he goes to work.

> "Remember the trick you used on Aunt Angie that summer we stayed with her? You rigged the doorknob so it wouldn't close securely when she tried to lock us in our room at night. We could do something like that."

This is an info dump because both characters already know the specifics. They'd be more likely to say...

> "What if you did what you used to do to Aunt Angie?"

The problem is that's not enough info for the reader.

So we pull out what's essential. When they were with Aunt Angie doesn't matter. Why she locked them up doesn't matter. What's really essential for the reader to know is that one brother knows how to rig a door so that even when it looks locked, it can actually be forced open.

> "What if you did what you used to do to Aunt Angie?"

Frank crinkled his forehead. "He never leaves us alone long enough. It took me a whole day to file the ridges off the doorknob latch."

But sometimes you really do need a character to talk about something they wouldn't normally talk about or to say something the listener already knows. What then?

Pick a fight.

Fighting characters will dredge up things the other character already knows and use them as weapons against each other.

Let's go back to our earlier example of the husband and wife (Nathan and Linda) who bought the house two years ago, drained their savings, and haven't been able to replace their savings yet. Say we have a scene happening where the husband finally quit the high-paying job where he's treated like a doormat, but he did it without talking to his wife first. She's angry because they won't be able to make their mortgage payments on her salary alone.

> Nathan balled up the resignation letter. "You're the one who wanted this house in the first place. I was happy in our apartment."
>
> "We bumped into each other just trying to dress in the morning. We couldn't raise a family there."
>
> "We could have waited at least. We shouldn't have rushed into a house and drained our savings. I wanted to stay in the job I loved."
>
> "So it's all my fault?" Linda grabbed a club from his golf bag by the door. "We'd have plenty saved if you'd give up a golf game now and then."

Same information, much more exciting way of sharing it. (We also learn more about the characters and their relationship.)

Introduce a character to "play dumb."

A "dumb" character is one who's new to the situation and doesn't know what the others do. They don't actually have to be unintelligent. They can be highly intelligent in other areas. They just need to be out of their element or uneducated in this particular scenario. (Jeff Gerke, editor-in-chief of Marcher Lord Press, calls this a dump puppet.)

In the movie *Twister*, Dr. Melissa Reeves functions in this role because she doesn't know anything about tornadoes. She asks questions no other character would ask because they already know all about tornadoes. Through her, we learn the information we need to learn.

This was also part of the brilliance in how J.K. Rowling wrote her *Harry Potter* stories. Even though Harry was born from magical parents, he knew nothing of the magical world prior to coming to Hogwarts because he was raised by Muggles (non-magical folk). In other words, Harry learned about the world at the same time we did, and gave Rowling a natural, believable way to tell us what we needed to know.

Often you can also use a child in this role because children are naturally curious and haven't yet developed the social filter that holds many adults back. My best friend's seven-year-old daughter once said to another woman, "I love your skirt. It looks just like a towel." Children can get away with things that adults can't.

CATCH-UP DIALOGUE

Catch-up dialogue is a unique situation because it's almost the flip of As-You-Know-Bob Syndrome. Instead of a character telling another character something they already know for the sake of the reader, it's a character telling another character something the reader already knows for the sake of that other character.

We've all hit those points where the reader has watched the scene play out, but now the character must return to his allies and tell them what went on. If he doesn't tell his allies, how will they know what happened? Catch-up dialogue can be necessary at times, but because the reader already knows about what one character is telling another, it's boring.

How do we manage catch up dialogue?

Add a new level of tension by leaving out a key detail.

Has your character forgotten something important that changes the nature of what they're saying? Are they leaving something out on purpose to protect one of the other characters? Are they leaving out something because they don't completely trust their allies or because they're watching out for their own interests rather than the interests of the group?

Summarize through indirect dialogue.

This is the easiest, smoothest, and least intrusive option.

"I wasn't sure I was going to make it out alive." I told them how I escaped. "But we need to keep moving. Once they figure out I'm gone, they'll be after us."

While this is telling rather than showing, it's one of the kinds of telling that's permissible in fiction.

TAKE IT TO THE PAGE

Option A Path

Step 1 - Check your green highlights for As-You-Know-Bob Syndrome. (By this point, if you've been highlighting physical pages, you may need to start from a fresh copy if you've already made major changes to your dialogue.) Can you bring in the information more naturally through writing a scene to showcase it, picking a fight, or using a character who's new to the situation?

Step 2 – Check your highlights for areas where catch-up dialogue might be making your scene feel slow or repetitive. Can you add a new element to it? If not, summarize it in indirect dialogue rather than having your reader sit through it again.

Option B Path

Step 1 – Use the skimming technique you should have perfected after the last chapter to check for As-You-Know-Bob Syndrome. Can you bring in the information more naturally through writing a scene to showcase it, picking a fight, or using a character who's new to the situation?

Step 2 – Go to the scenes where you think you might have used catch-up dialogue. Can you add a new element to it? If not, change it to indirect dialogue rather than having your reader sit through it again.

CHAPTER FIVE

Writing Dialogue Unique to Your Characters

I f you've been told your characters seem flat, sometimes the problem isn't that you haven't fully developed your characters. Sometimes it's the way you're writing their dialogue.

Your characters might all sound like you (or an idealized version or you). They might all sound like each other.

Here's how to set them apart.

THE REGIONALISMS FROM WHERE YOUR CHARACTER GREW UP OR NOW LIVES

Small touches in word choice make a big difference. Take me and my husband as examples. I'm a Canadian from Southwestern Ontario. My husband is an American from Virginia, just outside of Washington, DC.

I say pop – He says soda.

I say supper – He says dinner.

I say chocolate bar – He says candy bar.

I say house coat – He says bathrobe.

Along with small differences in word choice, characters from different regions will have different catch words. Stephen King's characters from Maine say *Ayuh* as an affirmative. Canadians will use *eh* as both an affirmative and a question, depending on the situation. In Western Indiana, people often drop *to be* from their sentences, so instead of "Your jeans need to be washed" they say "Your jeans need washed."

If you're going to use a regionalism, make sure you understand it properly or you're going to disgust a large portion of your readers.

In the movie *Argo*, based on a declassified true story, CIA agent Tony Mendez (Ben Affleck) goes into Iran, posing as a Canadian film producer to try to sneak six trapped Americans out. Thanks to the help of the Canadians, the six Americans now have Canadian passports, and Mendez spends hours quizzing them on their new identities. One mistake could mean capture and death.

He asks one of the six where they were born.

"Tor-on-to," the man answers.

Mendez corrects him. Canadians drop the second T, pronouncing it as Tor-on-no.

A small detail, but for every Canadian watching, that detail helps make the movie. Not pronouncing *Toronto* correctly is a dead giveaway to us that someone isn't really Canadian, and the writers took the time to research that.

Thanks to the Internet, there's no excuse for not contacting someone who lives in the region you're writing about and asking them for some tips.

If you're a science-fiction or fantasy author, regionalisms can be a goldmine for adding depth to your world. For example, does a regionalism give away a character's real nationality? Does it show that a character grew up in a poor region even though they now have money or standing?

In my co-written novel *The Amazon Heir*, Zerynthia, the Amazon protagonist, has no word for *brother*. In her society, all male babies are killed, so brothers don't exist. The closet she can come is saying *son of your father*.

YOUR CHARACTER'S EDUCATION LEVEL, IQ, AND STATION IN LIFE

While even the most highly educated among us rarely uses perfect grammar when we speak, grammatical errors, strategically used, say much about a character.

The character who says "I didn't see nobody" isn't the same as the character who says "I didn't see anyone."

A character who's highly educated or well-read will also naturally drop ten-dollar words or references to classic literature into their speech occasionally. Don't overuse this and send your readers running for a dictionary...or away from your book. As with grammatical errors, choose your spots for maximum impact.

What if your character's first language isn't English?

My grandparents were born in Slovakia (the poor, rural side of what used to be Czechoslovakia). My grandpa spoke no English when he first came to Canada, and he struggled because Slovakian is different from English in a very fundamental way. It depends on changing the ending of a word to indicate the word's function in a sentence rather than on word order. According to my grandma, he would make mistakes like saying, "Throw the cow over the fence to some hay."

Non-native English speakers also struggle with definite and indefinite article usage ("the" "a") and subject-verb agreement.

If you have a character who wasn't born in an English-speaking country, you can play with these issues (again, use a light hand) to set their dialogue apart.

If you're a science-fiction or fantasy author, do your races speak different languages? If you don't have a *Star Trek*-esque universal translator, how will you handle this?

YOUR CHARACTER'S TONE, PACE, AND VOLUME OF SPEECH

Is your character a fast or a slow talker? Do they speak softly or loudly? Is her voice high-pitched? Does he sound like a bass drum? Does he have a gravelly voice like Bill Pulman?

Your point-of-view character isn't going to notice these things about herself. To convey these details, wait until you're in someone else's point of view or make it believable for your POV character to think about her voice.

For example, your character sees an older couple from her church shuffling home, stops, and offers to give them a ride. They protest.

> I turned on my four-ways and hopped out of the car. Hopefully they wouldn't notice the empty soda bottles shoved under my seat. "No problem. I'm happy to help."
> The old man frowned. "What?"
> I tried again, louder.

The woman patted me on the arm. "Even if you yelled 'til your throat hurt, your voice is too high-pitched. He can't hear our grandchildren, either."

YOUR CHARACTER'S PERSONAL VOCABULARY

Does your character have a catchphrase?

Most of us do have certain phrases we default to. I use *cheesed* as a stand-in for *annoyed* or *peeved,* as in "If I get there and the store is closed, I'm going to be cheesed." Don't overuse habitual phrases, but they can add a nice distinctiveness when used strategically.

What words won't your character say?

Growing up, I knew another child who refused to say the word *condiments* because he'd accidentally called them *condoms* once and was both laughed at and punished. Does she avoid longer words for fear she'll use them wrong? Does she prefer pseudo-swear words to the actual thing?

Does your character use crutch words?

Crutch words are the ones that make grammar Nazis cringe. I'll give you three as examples.

Literally – *Literally* is often used to add hyperbole to a sentence. Because it means that something took place in the strictest sense, it can make for some humorous sentences.

"My head literally exploded."

"I walked a hundred miles to get there. Literally."

You can use this to your advantage not only as a crutch word to characterize a character, but also as a means to characterize a snarky or sarcastic character through their reply.

> "My head literally exploded when I saw all the papers piled on my desk."
> "That must have been messy."

Obviously – *Obviously* should only be used to describe an action that is easily observable, recognized, or understood. Not everyone uses it that way. A character who wants to make a point, cut off any disagreement, or who is a touch arrogant will use it for things that aren't cut and dry.

> "Obviously he shouldn't have bought that car. Everyone knows they're lemons."

Honestly – *Honestly* often gets used to try to add veracity to a statement. A character who feels like her word is always questioned might take to adding in this crutch word.

> "I honestly don't know why she did that."

Does your character use slang, jargon, or acronyms?

As a writer, you're probably used to talking about your WIP or MS. You know about NaNoWriMo and ARCs. But a non-writer isn't going to know that you mean work-in-progress and manuscript. They won't know that NaNoWriMo is short for National Novel Writing Month and that it takes place in November. They won't know that ARCs are advanced reader copies given out before a book is available for sale in the hope of building reviews and word of mouth.

Every sub-group has their own terminology—teachers, nurses, police, artists, surfers, and swing dancers. Sometimes their unique vocabulary even varies by what part of the world the group is located in. Worse, it changes over time. Surfers don't talk about "hanging ten" anymore.

Use slang, jargon, or acronyms with a very light hand because your reader probably won't understand them. Whenever possible, make sure you clarify for them.

YOUR CHARACTER'S PERSONALITY

Is your character the kind who always sticks their foot in their mouth?

Are they well-meaning or just so self-absorbed that they don't realize they've said something stupid? What do they do after they stick their foot in their mouth? Do they apologize and try to explain, or do they try to laugh it off?

Is your character confident or does she second-guess herself?

A confident character makes definitive statements. A character who second-guesses herself will add qualifiers—*I think, maybe, most.* They'll end their statements with a subtle request for reassurance—*Right? Eh? Don't you think?* She'll also ask questions rather than giving her opinion directly—*Do you think that couch might look better over there?* rather than *The couch would look better over there.* A character who's unsure of herself will also frequently apologize.

Does your character have a problem with authority? Are they a control freak? Or are they naturally curious about the way things work?

These types of characters will want to know the *why* and the reasons behind something rather than accepting what's said at face value.

Is your character a gossip?

Why is he or she a gossip? Is it because they care about the lives of others? Is it because they're easily bored? Is it because they have low self-esteem and want to find ways to tear others down so they can build themselves up?

Does he jump to conclusions?

If yes, is it because they're impatient, believe in their gut, or believe the worst of everyone? If no, is it because they're methodical and patient, or because they've had bad experiences with premature conclusions in the past and now their confidence is shattered?

Is your character a concrete thinker or an abstract thinker?

I'm not talking about psychological development here, but rather how we naturally think about and make sense of the world. A concrete thinker prefers to talk about what *is* rather than what *might be*. They don't enjoy plays on words. They take things literally. An abstract thinker takes what is and projects into the future what might be. They enjoy puns and word plays, and if you listen to them explain a concept, they'll often use metaphors. Many writers are abstract thinkers and don't realize that there's another way of thinking.

Is your character polite or blunt?

A polite character will look for a careful way to phrase something, often sugarcoating hard truths. A blunt character isn't going to care. They call it like they see it.

Is your character impatient? Is she a bully?

Both impatient characters and bullies are likely to cut people off. Bullies will also stoop to manipulation and verbal abuse.

Does he feel the need to defend himself against real or imagined slights?

You've probably met someone like this. They're always on the defensive even against the simplest statements, probably because they feel misunderstood or looked down on, or because at one time they were belittled or blamed for everything that went wrong. A defensive character likely has low self-esteem.

> Extra Tip: Whenever possible, carefully craft your character's first line of dialogue. It's part of the first impression he or she will make on your reader.

TAKE IT TO THE PAGE

Option A Path

Step 1 – Check each of your scenes. Could you delete a character and give their lines to someone else without a problem? Delete one of the characters in those scenes unless they're essential to the scene for another reason.

Step 2 – Is your story set in a location where you've never lived? Don't assume the regional speech quirks will be the same. Reach out on social media or use the resources in the next chapter to make sure your dialogue fits the area and time period in which your book is set.

Step 3 – Do you have a character whose first language isn't English? (Or whatever the primary language of your world might be.) Is their grammar too perfect? If they've been in the country long enough to sound like a native English speaker, could you have them slip up during times of stress?

Step 4 – For at least your main character, love interest, and antagonist, answer the questions under "Your Character's Personal Vocabulary" and "Know Your Character's Personality." Compare what you've discovered to major scenes. Do each character's passages reflect their personality? If not, make the necessary changes. If you want, you can also complete this step for other major characters. (I recommend doing it for any characters who play a significant role in the story.)

Step 5 – In Step 4, you worked on creating distinct dialogue for your most important characters. You probably won't want to do this for every character, especially the ones who only appear in one or two scenes. It's not a good investment of your time. Here's what you can do instead.

- ✓ Pick one minor character. Can you add some regional touches to help their dialogue stand out from your other minor characters?
- ✓ Pick a different character. Think about the ideas in "Your Character's Education Level, IQ, and Station in Life." Use these concepts to help make the speech of this character distinctly theirs.
- ✓ Pick another character. Can you set their dialogue apart using the ideas in "Your Character's Tone, Pace, and Volume of Speech"?
- ✓ Pick a fourth character, and use the prompts in "Your Character's Personal Vocabulary" to give uniqueness to their dialogue.

Go through and weave in the changes based on this exercise. It's okay if a walk-on-walk-off character isn't memorable as long as they serve their designated purpose in the story, but by setting at least a few of them apart, you'll make your world seem more realistic and eliminate wallpaper characters.

Step 6 – Write down the first line of dialogue spoken by your main character, their love interest, and the antagonist. Could you make those lines better and more memorable? Could you write them in a way that gives the reader an immediate picture of the character? Or could you use them to mislead your reader about the antagonist?

Option B Path

Step 1 – Quickly count up how many characters you have who receive only minor speaking parts. Could you cut a quarter of them and allow another character to fill their role and speak their lines? Do it.

Step 2 – Read through the sections on "Your Character's Personal Vocabulary" and "Know Your Character's Personality." Can you answer the questions for your main character, love interest, and antagonist? (You don't have to write down your answers if you don't want, though it can be very helpful to have a written guide, especially if you're writing a series.) If you can't answer the questions, or you find yourself answering them the same way for all three characters, jot down some point form notes on how you can set their dialogue apart. Choose five to six major scenes and apply these changes.

Step 3 – Do you have a character whose first language isn't English? (Or whatever the primary language of your world might be.) Is their grammar too perfect? If they've been in the country long enough to sound like a native English speaker, could you have them slip up during times of stress?

Step 4 – Write down the first line of dialogue spoken by your main character, their love interest, and the antagonist. Could you make those lines better and more memorable?

Could you write them in a way that gives the reader an immediate picture of the character? Or could you use them to mislead your reader about the antagonist?

Step 5 – When you've finished with your book and are trying to find beta readers or an editor, look for people who might live in (or at least be familiar with) the region in which your book is set. Let them know before they start that you'd like them to pay attention to whether or not your dialogue sounds authentic to where it's supposed to take place. (Please note: This isn't the most important qualification for an editor—it's more like a bonus.)

Important: Option A and Option B

Everything in this chapter can be done before you start writing your next book if you like to plan in advance.

CHAPTER SIX

Common Dialogue Challenges

Even if you're normally confident when it comes to writing dialogue, these questions can give us hives as we struggle to find answers. Some of them are easier to deal with than you might think.

WHAT DO WE DO ABOUT A CHARACTER WHO SPEAKS IN A PARTICULAR DIALECT?

The classic example of how not to do dialect is *Uncle Tom's Cabin* by Harriett Beecher Stowe. The passage below is Aunt Chloe speaking to Tom.

> "S'pose we must be resigned; but oh Lord! how ken I? If I know'd anything whar you's goin', or how they'd sarve you! Missis says she'll try and 'deem ye, in a year or two; but Lor! nobody never comes up that goes

down thar! They kills 'em! I've hearn 'em tell how dey works 'em up on dem ar plantations." (Chapter 10: "The Property Is Carried Off")

Dialect written out phonetically like this is a bad idea for many reasons. It's frustrating to your reader. You don't want anyone to have to work that hard just to understand what your characters are saying. It pulls them out of the fictional dream. Beyond this, dialect used in this way sounds forced and can even border on demeaning to whatever group you're trying to imitate.

So how do we find the balance between authenticity and readability?

Just name it.

> She had a heavy New York accent.

> He sounded like he was from the Deep South.

Is this telling rather than showing? Yes, but it's one of the situations where it's actually okay to tell. In fact, if you don't know how to replicate a dialect well enough to do it correctly, this is the wise option.

This technique works most successfully if you're choosing to name an accent your reader will immediately be able to call to mind.

Filter it through the ears of another character who's unfamiliar with the dialect.

I personally love when an author does this well, but it only works if your character isn't familiar with the dialect.

Jim glared at her. "You spoiled him. And after all, that ain't no real kindness." It came out like *Ya spiled 'im. And arter all, t'aint no real kindness.*

You don't have to do this more than once for the reader to understand what your character sounds like when they're speaking.

Also notice how adding a few select grammatical mistakes can also help convey the idea without having to transcribe the dialect. More on that in a second.

Point out a distinctive word here and there.

This option works in the same situations as the one above.

"I'm sorry," she said. "I didn't realize."
When she said *sorry*, it sounded like *soar-y* instead of *sari*. I couldn't get past the mental image of her covered in seeping wounds.

Forget copying it exactly, and instead think in terms of rhythm, word choice, syntax, grammatical mistakes, and missing words.

Abileen's chapters in *The Help* by Kathryn Stockett could be a master's class in this.

She uses *a* instead of *of*.

I done, not *I have*.

Them and *they* instead of *those* and *their*.

Small but important grammatical mistakes.

Stockett chooses the word *mamas* over *mothers*. She chooses *toilet bowl* rather than *potty* or *bathroom*.

Syntax is basically about the patterns that form sentences and phrases. Stockett also reverses the normal and expected order within Abileen's sentences. Go read even just the first page of the first chapter and you'll see what I mean.

And when you write dialect this way, you'll not only make the read easy and more immersive for your audience, you'll also avoid stereotypes and condescension.

A good source for preliminary dialect research is http://dialectblog.com. You can also find a map at http://aschmann.net/AmEng/ that breaks down all of North America by linguistic patterns and includes recordings. For more audio examples, you can browse the Speech Accent Archive created by George Mason University at http://accent.gmu.edu/.

WHAT DO WE DO ABOUT A CHARACTER WHO STUTTERS OR HAS A LISP?

In the 2001 movie *Pearl Harbor*, the character Red has a severe stutter. It's painful to listen to because you so desperately want to help him force the words out. If you overdo stuttering or lisping in your novel, though, your readers will have that same experience and might find it so frustrating or annoying that they give up.

Better than making your reader struggle every time your character with a stutter or a lisp talks is to introduce it strategically at key moments or to use some of the techniques suggested earlier for dialect.

A speech impediment should never be the entirety of your characterization. Before you create a character who stutters or has a lisp, ask yourself what it will contribute to the story. Why do you want it there? How is it connected to the rest of the plot?

You also want to be sure you know enough about these speech impediments to portray them accurately, in a truthful rather than stereotypical or demeaning way.

IS THERE A LIMIT ON HOW OFTEN A CHARACTER SHOULD USE PROFANITY?

Like contractions in certain genres, profanity is a divisive topic. Some people see it as unnecessary and lazy writing. Other people see it as a mark of realism and pepper their writing with so much you couldn't read a single line out loud to your three-year-old.

If you frequently use profanity in your writing, understand that you'll lose readers you could have kept by cutting it (or at least toning it down).

You might think I'm being extreme, but I've put down books, never to pick them up again and never to read the author again, because of the amount of swearing. I know people who skim a book before buying it, looking for how many times swear words are used in a chapter. Many book reviewers state they won't review books with profanity.

Just because you're comfortable with it doesn't mean everyone will be. Perhaps this doesn't matter because you know your ideal reader won't mind. Whatever you decide, make sure it's a conscious choice you've thought about rather than just what you defaulted to.

As you could probably guess, I advise you to use profanity sparingly in your writing. Here are my tips for handling it.

Use indirect dialogue instead.

If your only reason for including profanity is for shock value, leave it out and use indirect dialogue instead.

> John cursed. "What did they think they were doing?"

Still realistic but not offensive to readers.

Earn them.

Too often the charge that profanity is lazy writing, used to prop up weak dialogue, is true. So if you want to use profanity, treat it like a rite of passage. Add it in only if you've already written strong dialogue that could stand without it.

Use profanity to make a point.

When someone swears constantly, the power of those words vanishes. It becomes like talking to someone who only ever speaks in a monotone. If you use profanity constantly, how do you emphasize something when you really need to? You also lose the opportunity to characterize by having a character only swear when they're angry, frightened, or joking.

Make sure they're situation-appropriate.

Not even a Marine uses the same language around his priest or grandmother that he uses in the field. Most people don't swear with the same intensity at the office as they do at a football game.

Understand that you can be realistic without using an abundance of profanity.

Do you remember all the ways we talked about to get around dialect? Writing a story where dialogue isn't spelled out phonetically doesn't weaken the story. In fact, most of the time, it makes it stronger. It's up to you to decide whether the same is true about profanity in your novel.

> Extra Tip: Science-fiction and fantasy writers, all of this applies to your made-up profanity as well. Use it strategically, as a means of characterization and world-building. When done well, invented profanity can even sneak into popular usage (like the new F-word in *Battlestar Galactica*).

IN HISTORICAL FICTION, HOW DO WE MANAGE TO KEEP OUR DIALOGUE TRUE TO THE TIME PERIOD WITHOUT ALLOWING IT TO SOUND STILTED?

I asked this question to award-winning historical romance author Jody Hedlund.

You can read Jody's full answer by entering her name into the search box on my website, but in a nutshell, she said, "I don't try to imitate the time period speech exactly. I usually pick out distinct words and assign them to particular characters to use throughout the book."

When in doubt about whether a word is too modern, look it up. Jody suggested Phrases.org.uk as her go-to. Dictionary.com will also often tell you when a word originated. You don't have to stick solely to words from the era you're writing about, but the closer you can come, the better.

A word might also sound too modern even if it isn't. Occasionally you're going to run into a word that's ancient but sounds modern. Technically you're correct in using it, but I'd recommend changing it. Not all readers are historical scholars. They go by what sounds right.

SHOULD WE USE CONTRACTIONS IN SCIENCE FICTION, FANTASY, AND HISTORICAL FICTION?

In every critique group, fiction intensive, or mentorship class I've ever attended with other fantasy, science-fiction, and historical fiction writers, this question has come up. And the class divided down the middle on the answer.

Those who felt contractions were acceptable argued that taking them out made the writing sound stilted and awkward. Those who felt contractions were unacceptable argued that using them made the writing sound inauthentic and modern.

However, most languages, even ancient ones, had a way of shortening words, or slang that made certain words and phrases easier and quicker to say.

Patricia T. O'Connor and Stewart Kellerman point out in their book *Origins of the Specious: Myths and Misconceptions of the English Language* that Old English used contractions. For example, *ne is* ("is not") contracted to *nis* ("isn't") and *ne wolde* ("would not") contracted to *nolde* ("wouldn't"). In other words, contractions aren't a modern construct.

Contractions have gone in and out of fashion over the years, more so in writing than in speech. Even among the upper classes, contractions would have been used and tolerated in speech when they were considered unacceptable in writing.

So where does that leave us? We need to always strive for dialogue that sounds smooth and natural. If an excessive removal of contractions leaves our work feeling stilted and awkward, we should look for other ways to give an authentic feel.

We can instead rearrange the syntax of our sentences. We can remove contractions at key moments for emphasis (and downplay them throughout). We can replace modern-feeling phrases with ones slightly less common.

WHAT DO WE DO ABOUT A CHARACTER WHO IS THE STRONG, SILENT TYPE?

Strong, silent types can be more difficult for the reader to get to know, but they don't have to be. The trick to creating a good strong, silent character is consistency between their personality and their actions.

A strong, silent type will express their opinions through their actions, rather than through their words, whenever possible.

If someone insults the woman this character loves, he won't yell or even issue an order. He'll pick the guy up by the collar and toss him out the door. Or he'll hit him.

If your strong, silent type is in love, he's likely to show it through rotating his love interest's tires or volunteering to go on the quest for whatever object she needs. He won't be eloquent in expressing his love, but you'll be able to see it.

If this type of character believes the corrupt government needs to be brought down, he's not going to form groups and start petitions. He's going to grab a gun (or phaser or sword) and attack.

A strong, silent type will only speak when they have something important to say.

They like to listen more than they speak. They won't banter or engage in small talk. They won't fill the air with their grandiose plans. They won't be generous with their praise. But when they say something, you'll want to listen. Make every piece of dialogue you give them matter, and the few things they say will count for as much as the pages you gave to the chatty fellow who's full of hot air.

A strong, silent type is likely to mean what they say and to act on it.

They won't make idle threats. In fact, they won't make threats at all. They'll make statements, and then they'll move directly from that into following through with what they just said. By the time this type of character speaks, they've already thought things through and made their decision, and they'll be difficult to stop. They won't ask permission.

Make a strong, silent type uncomfortable when he needs to talk about emotions or anything he'd consider private.

This type of character often has emotions that run deep, but he's not comfortable with sharing them, so if you do need him to open up, make sure it doesn't come easy for him. And make sure you have to drag those emotions out of him.

Another key to remember is that a strong, silent type won't share these emotions publicly. He's the type whose wife will die, and he won't shed a tear in public. He'll wait to grieve privately. Never have your strong, silent character open up when there are multiple people around. It should be one-on-one with someone he trusts.

IS IT ALRIGHT TO START A CHAPTER WITH DIALOGUE?

We've heard the rule "never start a scene with dialogue," but is this a hard rule, or does it have a little flex to it?

The main reason new writers are told to never start with a line of dialogue is that you leave the reader without context. They don't have the immediate grounding of knowing who's speaking, who they're speaking to, and where they are.

Reading is subjective. Some people (like me) won't mind that. Others will immediately feel disconnected and won't be drawn in.

But we can create a dialogue opening that grounds people more quickly and makes for as strong an opening as any other.

Make this one of the strongest lines of dialogue in the entire book.

Cut the flab. Make it interesting even without context around it. Choose power words. (Power words are words that seem to almost come with their own emotional charge. *Menacing. Tears. Knife. Seduction. Gossip. Suspicion.* Margie Lawson covers power words in her Writer's Academy courses.)

Give a touch of context as soon as possible, and attach the dialogue to a person.

The sooner we know who's speaking and who they're speaking to, the better. By attaching a tag or a beat to a line of dialogue, it helps the reader understand what's going on.

Look how Elizabeth Spann Craig does this in her fifth Myrtle Clover cozy mystery, *Death at a Drop-In.*

> "Miles?" asked Myrtle, peering closely at her friend.
> "Are you asking me on a date?"

While we don't yet know the setting, we know a character named Myrtle is talking to her friend Miles, and that an invitation is in question. Because of the way Spann Craig grounds us, we're not confused at all.

A dialogue opening must relate directly to the plot.

In any opening, it's cheating the reader to start off with something exciting that will have absolutely no relation to the rest of the plot. It's even worse to do it with a dialogue opening. While you don't need to introduce the main conflict, you do need to give the reader a sense of the plot and characters that at least mirrors the central conflict.

An example you might want to check out is from Kelly Gay's *The Better Part of Darkness* (Charlie Madigan, Book 1). (Again, you should be able to see this using the preview feature from any online retailer who sells the book.)

In the opening sentence, you immediately know this is a fantasy, specifically an urban fantasy, thanks to the mention of both a two-thousand-year-old oracle and fast-food napkins, so the reader is grounded in the correct genre. You know that two characters named Hank and Charlie are involved, and you get a taste of their relationship. You also get a sense that the plot might revolve around problems with the normal world and the magical world getting along. This is exactly the case, since Charlie and Hank have to investigate the source of a new otherworldly narcotic, known as ash, that's killing the humans who use it.

When former literary agent Nathan Bransford took a poll on his blog about dialogue openings, he pointed out that dialogue openings are an advanced technique, separating those who've mastered their art from those who are still learning.

If you're not sure you have the skills for a great dialogue opening, you're better to open another way.

TAKE IT TO THE PAGE

Option A Path and Option B Path

For this chapter, there's no way to fast-track the process, so whether you're an Option A person or an Option B person, the work will be the same. If you're normally an Option B person, hang in there. It won't be as painful as you think. Promise.

Step 1 – Do you use dialect in your story? If you've written it out phonetically, change it. If you know the dialect you're trying to portray intimately (i.e., you speak it) or you have a good ear for languages and are willing to study the dialect you plan to use, rewrite your dialect using rhythm, word choice, syntax, grammatical mistakes, and missing words. Otherwise, you'd be better off using one of the less-invasive techniques to convey dialect.

Once you've written out your dialect using rhythm, word choice, syntax, etc., enlist the help of someone you trust to read a couple pages out loud to you. This is the best way to hear if you've achieved the effect you're looking for.

Step 2 – Do you have a character who stutters or has a lisp? Go through every chapter where that character appears and highlight in orange how often you include an indication of the stutter or lisp. Is it really necessary? Does its use in that particular passage indicate something about the character or his emotional state? If not, remove it. Try to remove three-quarters of the uses.

Step 3 – Have you used profanity in your fiction? Think about how and why you've chosen to use profanity in the way you have. Make sure what you've done is a conscious, well-thought-out choice. If you find yourself wanting to make changes, use the Find feature of your word-processing program to run a search for swear words. (It'll be easier than trying to find them all manually.)

Step 4 – Does your story include a strong, silent type? Mark all his or her passages of dialogue with a red pen (if you're an Option A person still working with their originally highlighted physical copy) or with purple highlighting if you're working on a computer copy.

- ✓ Make sure this character speaks less frequently than the others.
- ✓ Make sure you've made this character uncomfortable when it's absolutely necessary that he or she shares something private or deals with emotions.
- ✓ When this character speaks, have they said something truly worth saying?
- ✓ When this character speaks, could they have simply acted instead?

Step 5 – Check the first line of each chapter. Have you used any dialogue openings? If so, evaluate them against the criteria in this chapter and see if you can improve them.

Step 6 (For Historical Fiction Authors) – When you send your story to beta readers, when you're looking for a critique partner, or when you're thinking of hiring an editor, try to find someone who is familiar with other fiction written in the same time period. Let them know up front that the appropriateness of your dialogue to the time period is one thing you want them to watch for. For all your other early readers, ask them to flag any words that sound too modern to them. Even if they aren't familiar with the time period, they can tell you what sounds off to their ears.

Step 7 (For Science-Fiction, Historical Fiction, and Fantasy Authors) – How have you handled contractions in your work? If you've left them out for the most part, print off a copy of your story and record yourself reading it. Play it back and mark on your printed copy wherever it sounds stilted and you need to add a contraction to make it sound smoother. (Most laptops now come with a built in webcam and microphone, but if yours doesn't, or if you have a desktop computer, you can buy an inexpensive headset. Then all you need to do is download Audacity. It's a free program that will record straight onto your computer for you.)

Adding Tension to Your Dialogue

I n Chapter Two, we talked about how to add variety to your dialogue, and those techniques will add tension on the micro scale. There are also ways you can add tension on a macro scale using agendas, reticence to share, and arguments.

GIVE YOUR CHARACTER AN AGENDA

When we talk to others, we always have something we want from the conversation—that's our agenda. Talking, even for women, is never an end unto itself.

Perhaps we want the other person to do something for us, or we want to convince them of our point of view, or we want to find out a piece of information that's important to us, or we want to portray ourselves in a certain way. If nothing else, when we talk, we're seeking to bond, to feel heard, to receive reassurance, or to find the quickest possible way to exit the conversation without being rude.

We don't always make our agendas obvious to the people we're talking to however—at least at the start of the conversation.

Say you want to borrow money from your best friend. Would you leap right into the request or would you come at it indirectly by asking how their business is doing or whether they're expecting a big tax refund this year?

As a writer, you need to know each character's agenda in a conversation, even if you don't reveal it to the reader right away. Why? Well, you want your characters to have conflicting agendas for a conversation as often as possible.

If you have a wife whose agenda for a conversation is to feel heard and understood, and her husband spends the whole time they're talking checking his email, fiddling with his phone, or reading the sports page, the tension will build until the wife snaps.

In figuring out what each character's agenda is, it helps to remember that each character is the sun in their own solar system. They believe it's their story. That husband who seems indifferent to his wife who wants his attention might be trying to relax after a long day so he doesn't take his frustration out on her, or he might be trying to finish up the last bit of work so he can get to bed early and not fall asleep on his drive to work the next morning.

DON'T MAKE THEM TOO EAGER TO SHARE

Have you ever been in one of those awkward situations where someone you've just met shares too-intimate details of their life with you? It's as awkward in writing as it is in person. And most people don't do it.

Unless you've created a character who is a habitual over-sharer, make them reticent to share personal, private details with people they've just met. Letting the relationship evolve naturally gives your reader time to wonder and get to know your character.

You can bring your characters to the brink of sharing, have them hint; have them evade. Just don't give away too much until a strong enough relationship has developed between characters to warrant it.

ALLOW THEM TO ARGUE

Arguments are one of the most powerful—and most abused—dialogue tools. If we're told our dialogue is dull or our plot is slow, we'll throw in an argument to spice things up. But an argument for an argument's sake isn't going to help. If we want an argument to add tension, we need to do it right.

Make it matter to the plot.

Do you know someone who always seems to pick a fight just because they enjoy fighting? Don't be that person in writer form. Readers aren't going to care about your argument if it doesn't advance the plot. The argument needs to be meaningful (even if that meaning is couched in subtext).

Build on previous arguments and build toward future ones.

In life, fights we've had with that person in the past that weren't fully resolved feed into every new argument we have. When writing an argument, keep in mind the arguments and hurts that have come before and plant the seeds for the ones you want to have come after. Never let your characters come out unscathed.

Keep the argument on track.

If you read only the dialogue, you should be able to see how one line leads into the next. Don't let your characters get off on rabbit trails or argue in circles. Your argument needs to make sense to the reader, and not become boring by covering the same ground over and over again.

Have your characters fight in line with their personalities.

Our personalities influence everything we do, including our arguments. A person who bends the ethical lines in every other area of their life will fight dirty. The sweetie who hates to hurt anyone will fight fair, no name-calling, no low blows. The controller will guilt trip and manipulate. If you want to break with your characters' personalities, you need to have a good reason for it.

Don't give in too early.

In real life, we want an argument to finish because it's unpleasant and uncomfortable. In fiction, you want to stretch that tension your reader is feeling. Resolution shouldn't come easily or quickly. Even better if you can leave the argument only partially resolved until later on. Your arguments should also follow an arc the same way your plot does. Don't land your biggest blow too early in the argument or everything after it will feel anticlimactic.

Add context.

Arguments are exciting to write, so it's easy to get carried away until your characters are just talking heads in a void. Arguments in fiction are about balance. You need enough action to keep your characters grounded in the world around them, and enough internal monologue to let your readers feel the full impact of what's happening.

Balance give-and-take.

In the best arguments, as with the most exciting physical fights, the opponents should be evenly matched. Never allow one person to gain the upper hand for long. You want to keep the reader wondering who will win.

Vary your arguments.

Not every argument is a screaming match. Some of the most vicious arguments are spoken quietly, in subtext. Try to find a new way for your characters to fight rather than always having them yelling at each other. Try putting them in a location or situation where they can't argue in the same way they've argued in the past.

TAKE IT TO THE PAGE

Option A Path

Step 1 – For every significant conversation (i.e., ones that last for more than a couple of sentences), write a note on your paper copy or make a comment using the comment feature in your word processing program about what each character wants to achieve from the conversation. If your characters in each conversation don't have conflicting agendas, can you give them conflicting agendas?

Step 2 – Identify the significant revelations in your story. Can you add tension to your story by pushing back a significant revelation? Think about this change before actually making it, though. There is such a thing as withholding a revelation too long. If you push the revelation back, would it improve your plot and pacing?

Step 3 – Highlight every argument in your story. Ask yourself the following questions.
- ✓ Does it matter to the plot?
- ✓ How have previous arguments influenced this argument? What future argument does this one set up?
- ✓ Does your argument make sense if you read only the dialogue?
- ✓ Does each character's style of fighting match their personality?

✓ Do your characters give up too easily? If this issue is important to them, they should "fight to the death." If it isn't important enough for them to really battle it out, why have you included the argument?
✓ Do you have too many "naked" lines of dialogue without internal dialogue or action breaking them up?
✓ Are the combatants evenly matched? If not, how could you even the odds?
✓ Is this argument identical in style to the previous arguments (even if the content is different)?

Option B Path

Step 1 – Skim each significant conversation (i.e., ones that last for more than a couple of sentences). Is there conflict in each of these conversations? If not, give the characters involved conflicting agendas.

Step 2 – Identify the significant revelations in your story. Can you add tension to your story by pushing back a significant revelation? Think about this change before actually making it, though. There is such a thing as withholding a revelation too long. If you push the revelation back, would it improve your plot and pacing?

Step 3 – Pick three to five arguments from your story and answer the following questions.
✓ Does it matter to the plot?
✓ How have previous arguments influenced this argument? What future argument does this one set up?

- ✓ Does your argument make sense if you read only the dialogue?
- ✓ Does each character's style of fighting match their personality?
- ✓ Do your characters give up too easily? If this issue is important to them, they should "fight to the death." If it isn't important enough for them to really battle it out, why have you included the argument?
- ✓ Do you have too many "naked" lines of dialogue without internal dialogue or action breaking them up?
- ✓ Are the combatants evenly matched? If not, how could you even the odds?
- ✓ Is this argument identical in style to the previous arguments (even if the content is different)? How could you change things up?

CHAPTER EIGHT

Where the Art of Dialogue Meets the Science

N ot everything can be summed up in easy rules, patterns, or formulae when it comes to dialogue (or anything in writing, for that matter).

It's part science, part art.

This chapter is about the higher-level techniques of dialogue that I call "art" because your ability to master them develops the more you write. I can give you guidelines to follow, and then it's up to you to hone your ear and your instincts.

DON'T MAKE DIALOGUE TOO FORMAL

If you talk to someone who knows me in real life, they'll tell you I'm a bit of a grammar Nazi. I tell you that to add context to what I say next.

Dialogue is one place where you'll rarely use perfect grammar. Even I don't speak in grammatically perfect English. Because we rarely have time to carefully construct a sentence before we speak it, mistakes sneak in. Few people know the rules of grammar well enough to always speak without mistakes, and those who do frequently come off as pretentious.

Sentence fragments are also acceptable, and expected, in dialogue. Most of us speak in sentence fragments as often (or more often) than we speak in complete sentences.

Dialogue is also someplace you want to liberally use contractions. Dialogue with contractions sounds more natural and less forced.

The exception to this is if you want to hint that a character is lying. People who are lying tend to remove contractions from their speech. In trying to convince you of the truth of their words, they add emphasis by removing the contractions.

I most commonly see the error of dialogue that's too formal in people with formal training (for example, people who majored in English or history in university). Remember that what you're writing isn't an essay. It's not a scholarly journal article. It's an imitation of life, and life is nothing if not imperfect.

JOHN SAID VS. SAID JOHN

I often advise newer writers to always write *John said*, never *said John*. You'll frequently find the latter in classic literature, but it went out of style decades ago. And this is one style that won't be coming back. The former is standard now.

If you're a newer writer, I'd still advise you to stick to *John said*.

However, once in a while, *said John* just sounds better. The problem is your ear needs to develop before you'll be able to reliably hear when that's the case. It's about rhythm rather than rules.

When are the most common times you might want to consider *said John*?

Scenes with multiple speakers.

I most commonly find this happening in a scene with three or more speakers, when you have two of the characters speaking and a third jumps in.

> Jared measured out in two-finger spacings what remained of the bread. "We can't stay here any longer."
> "How many days do we have left?" Randy asked.
> "Two at most."
> "We could stretch it to three," said Ellie. "It wouldn't hurt any of us to lose some weight."

When you listen to it, it's almost as if the switch throws things off just enough that it mimics the unbalance Ellie's interruption adds to the conversation.

When you need to quickly establish how something was said rather than who said it.

If you're going to tag a sentence that isn't simply said, it can sometimes be more important to put the quality of the speech first because that's what you want the reader to know as soon as possible.

> Sarah yanked him away from the loose shale. "Clumsy oaf. You'll have every tracker within ten miles on our trail."
> "Let them come!" shouted Dave.

This isn't something you always have to do. You definitely don't want to overdo it. But sometimes it works.

Don't break the *John said* "rule" just because you can. If you want to break it, make sure you have a good reason. Listen for alliteration, monotonous tag patterns, where the emphasis needs to fall in a sentence, and whether it's more important to quickly establish who's speaking or how it was spoken. All of those issues will help you decide if it might be right to at least bend the rule.

HOW TO HANDLE SCENES WITH MULTIPLE SPEAKERS

Scenes with multiple speakers can quickly get tricky. You need to identify who's speaking well enough that the reader isn't confused. If they have to stop and think about who's speaking, you've jerked them out of the story. As writers, we never want that to happen.

The obvious way to fix this is to make sure every line of dialogue is clearly tagged, but too many tags can leave the scene feeling clunky, as we discussed earlier. Adding beats in place of tags can help add variety, but there are two other ways we can help keep the speaker straight.

Identify the speaker early.

Remember how in Chapter One we talked about including a tag or beat at the first natural pause in a longer section of dialogue? This early identification becomes even more important if you have multiple people in a scene. Identify the speaker as early as possible if there's any chance of confusion.

Create a subset.

Imagine you're at a party, and you end up in a group of five people discussing holiday decorations. You're rarely going to find that all five people are engaging in the conversation equally at all times. Instead, what often happens is that two people will take over the conversation for a short period of time while the others listen.

This works great in fiction because, even though you have more than two people in the scene, you can have a back-and-forth exchange between two of them where you don't have to add an attribution to every line. Once you establish the pattern, until you break that pattern, the reader will assume that Line A is spoken by Dave, Line B by Sally, Line C by Dave, Line D by Sally, and so on.

VARY THE PATTERN OF TAGS AND BEATS

An all-or-nothing mentality will get you in trouble in most areas of life. Dialogue is no exception.

Dialogue tags and beats are both helpful. Overusing either leads to dialogue problems.

Too many *said* tags in a row results in either jerkiness or a monotonous pattern.

> "You might want to get caught, but I don't," Sarah said.
> "I'm just sick of running," Dave said.
> "Fine, but we should have decided together," Annie said.

Do you see how a tag that's normally invisible now draws attention to itself?

Overusing beats can be just as bad.

> Sarah shoved Dave. "You might want to get caught, but I don't."
> Dave planted his feet and crossed his arms over his chest. "I'm just sick of running."
> Annie rubbed her temples in slow circles. "Fine, but we should have decided together."

By adding variety, you can immediately make our little example better.

> Sarah shoved Dave. "You might want to get caught, but I don't."
> "I'm just sick of running."
> "Fine." Annie rubbed her temples in slow circles. "But we should have decided together."

While it would still need work, you've eliminated the problems inherent in going all-or-nothing on either beats or tags.

VARY THE LENGTH OF YOUR LINES

Another easy trap that can make your dialogue sound monotonous is lines of equal length.

> Dave says something using a sentence with nine words.
> Sarah replies with a sentence almost the exact same length.
> Annie follows with another sentence of equivalent length.

See how that can look and sound? It's flat.

> Dave says something using a sentence with nine words.
> Sarah snaps at him.

Annie tries to make amends with a defense of Sarah's actions. It takes a while. She's detailed.

Dave scowls.

The second sequence is much more interesting.

F-A-D (FEELING/ACTION/DIALOGUE)

Another common mistake is to place your beat (the action) after your dialogue. Beats almost always come before dialogue, and a character's emotions should precede the action beat. (I'll talk about an exception in the next section.)

I can feel you rebelling already against the idea that you need to follow a particular order of feeling, then action, then dialogue when you write. If you don't follow this pattern, though, your writing will feel off to your readers because you'll unintentionally violate the law of cause coming before effect (or action coming before reaction). In life, which fiction imitates, there's a natural order to things. Our job is to mimic that natural order.

In life, we have an emotional, instinctive, or reflexive reaction to an event first. It happens quickly and requires no conscious thought. We see a gun and fear shoots through our body.

These emotions cause us to act. Sometimes an action can be almost unconscious, a knee-jerk reaction to your feelings. We see a gun, fear shoots through our body, and we throw our hands in front of our face.

A thought can also be a reaction to an emotion. We see a gun, fear shoots through our body, and we think *I don't want to die.*

Finally, we speak because speech is externalizing what's going on inside. Speech, even when you're angry, generally takes longer and requires more mental engagement. It's a rational reaction.

Wrong:

> "I don't know why he would steal the cinnamon jelly beans." Emily shrugged.

Right:

> Emily shrugged. "I don't know why he would steal the cinnamon jelly beans."

Keep in mind that, like most writing "rules," you don't need to follow this 100% of the time, but you should follow it most of the time and only break it if you have a strong reason for doing so. ("That's how I saw it play out in my head" isn't a strong enough reason.)[1]

ADD A PAUSE IN THE MIDDLE OF A LINE OF DIALOGUE

Sometimes you'll notice a pattern like this appearing in your dialogue.

> Action. "Dialogue."
> "Dialogue," tag.
> Feeling. Action. "Dialogue."
> Action. "Dialogue."
> "Dialogue," tag.

---

[1] I learned the acronym F-A-D from agent Evan Marshall's book *The Marshall Plan for Novel Writing* (2001).

If this pattern goes on for too long, the lack of variety in structure can become boring regardless of how thrilling the content of your dialogue is. Often you can fix it by simply inserting a beat in the middle of two sentences of dialogue.

Original:

> Melody crossed her arms over her chest. "I don't like it here. I want to go home."

Revised:

> "I don't like it here." Melody crossed her arms over her chest. "I want to go home."

It adds a pause to the rhythm. You can feel Melody's hesitation.

When to add a beat and when to leave the dialogue straight is almost more a matter of instinct and hearing the cadence of your character's speech patterns than it is a scientific formula of tag here + beat there = interesting dialogue. You need to feel when your character might hesitate, pause, or take a breath.

> Extra Tip: This doesn't violate the concept of F-A-D. It's a variation of it. You'll notice that the beat isn't moved to the end of the dialogue, but is instead used as a pause in it, almost like the speaker is taking a breath—the same way we do in real life.

DON'T BREAK UP YOUR DIALOGUE TOO MUCH

Adding a beat to break up our dialogue can add the variety we need, but when done too often it can cause problems of its own.

As writers, we're tempted to write the scene the way we see it play out in our minds. Because that's how we see it, we fight changing it.

However, the way we imagine it in our heads isn't always the best way to put it down on paper.

A prime example of this is when we break up our dialogue with too many beats. We see our character moving around as they talk, so that's how we write it.

> "I can't see any way out." John peeped through the broken corner of the frosted window. "They're everywhere." He paced away from the window and back. "One of us will have to sacrifice ourselves to distract them." His shoulders slumped. "I don't suppose anyone wants to volunteer?"

It feels choppy. Occasionally this might be the effect you're going for, but you need to know you're doing it and use it strategically. Most of the time, you shouldn't break up your dialogue that much.

INDIRECT DIALOGUE

Indirect dialogue is summarized dialogue. It walks the tightrope between showing and telling, but it's an incredibly useful stylistic choice when used correctly.

I've already given you examples earlier in the book of specific times when indirect dialogue works well. (If you don't remember, glance back at the sections on swearing, catch-up dialogue, and dialect.) I haven't yet given you a general guideline to follow, though, so here it is.

Use indirect dialogue when the reader needs to know that a conversation is happening but doesn't need the blow-by-blow.

> Annie scrubbed at their muddy clothes hard enough to bruise her fingers against the stream rocks. Dave and Sally continued to bicker behind her. You'd think with their lives at stake they could lay off pushing each other's buttons for ten minutes.

In this situation, Dave and Sally nit-picking at each other is a common occurrence. We've probably heard enough of it earlier in the book, and we don't need to hear every word of it again. What's important here is that Annie's patience with their arguing is growing thin. Indirect dialogue works better here than direct dialogue to show that.

Never use indirect dialogue for an important conversation. If you summarize this type of conversation, your reader is going to feel held at a distance and cheated.

TAKE IT TO THE PAGE

Option A Path

Step 1 – Go through your book and highlight feelings in red, actions in yellow, and dialogue in green. Look at the color patterns in paragraphs with dialogue. It should be red, then yellow, then green, like an upside-down traffic light. (If a color is missing, that's fine. You don't need to use each element every time.) If the color pattern is wrong, it means you have a problem with your F-A-D sequences.

Step 2 – Read your dialogue out loud.
- ✓ Would you actually say it that way, or is your dialogue too formal?
- ✓ Pay attention to where you'd naturally pause, hesitate, or breathe. Try adding a beat in that spot to allow the reader to feel it.
- ✓ Do you hear a monotonous pattern forming? Vary up your tags and beats.

Step 3 – Zoom out enough that you can see the bigger picture, but stay close enough that you can see the words if need be.
- ✓ Is there enough variety in the length of your lines and size of your paragraphs?
- ✓ Look at the color patterns in the dialogue paragraphs. Do you have red (feelings) and yellow (action) breaking up your dialogue too often (potentially leading to a choppy feeling)?

Step 4 – Run a search for *shouted*, *whispered*, or other verbs denoting volume. Read the whole passage around them. Would it be better to switch the order so they come before the speaker's name?

Step 5 – Check your multiple-speaker scenes. Is it clear who's speaking, or do you find yourself confused?

Option B Path

Do the steps suggested for Option A people on two to three of your pages. Where are your problem areas? Focus on those steps.

Other Books by Marcy Kennedy

For Writers

Mastering Showing and Telling in Your Fiction

You've heard the advice "show, don't tell" until you can't stand to hear it anymore. Yet fiction writers of all levels still seem to struggle with it.

There are three reasons for this. The first is that this isn't an absolute rule. Telling isn't always wrong. The second is that we lack a clear way of understanding the difference between showing and telling. The third is that we're told "show, don't tell," but we're often left without practical ways to know how and when to do that, and how and when not to. So that's what this book is about.

Chapter One defines showing and telling and explains why showing is normally better.

Chapter Two gives you eight practical ways to find telling that needs to be changed to showing and guides you in understanding how to make those changes.

Chapter Three explains how telling can function as a useful first draft tool.

Chapter Four goes in-depth on the seven situations when telling might be the better choice than showing.

Chapter Five provides you with practical editing tips to help you take what you've learned to the pages of your current novel or short story.

Mastering Showing and Telling in Your Fiction: A Busy Writer's Guide also includes three appendices covering how to use *The Emotion Thesaurus*, dissecting an example so you can see the concepts of showing vs. telling in action, and explaining the closely related topic of As-You-Know-Bob Syndrome.

Strong Female Characters (A Mini-Book)

The misconceptions around what writers mean when we talk about strong female characters make them one of the most difficult character types to write well. Do we have to strip away all femininity to make a female character strong? How do we keep a strong female character likeable? If we're writing historical fiction or science fiction or fantasy based on a historical culture, how far can we stray from the historical records when creating our female characters?

In *Strong Female Characters: A Busy Writer's Guide* you'll learn

- what "strong female characters" means,
- the keys to writing characters who don't match stereotypical male or female qualities,
- how to keep strong female characters likeable, and
- what roles women actually played in history.

How to Write Faster (A Mini-Book)

In *How to Write Faster: A Busy Writer's Guide* you'll learn eight techniques that can help you double your word count in a way that's sustainable and doesn't sacrifice the quality of your writing in favor of quantity.

In our new digital era, writers are expected to produce multiple books and short stories a year, and to somehow still find time to build a platform through blogging and social media. We end up burning out or sacrificing time with our family and friends to keep up with what's being asked of us.

How to Write Faster provides you with tools and tips to help you find ways to write better, faster, and still have fun doing it, so that you'll have time left to spend on living life away from your computer. This book was written for writers who believe that there's more to life than just the words on the page and who want to find a better balance between the work they love and living a full life. The best way to do that is to be more productive in the writing time we have.

Fiction

Frozen: Two Suspenseful Short Stories

Twisted sleepwalking.

A frozen goldfish in a plastic bag.

And a woman afraid she's losing her grip on reality.

"A Purple Elephant" is a suspense short story about grief and betrayal.

In "The Replacements," a prodigal returns home to find that her parents have started a new family, one with no room for her. This disturbing suspense short story is about the lengths to which we'll go to feel like we're wanted, and how we don't always see things the way they really are.

ABOUT THE AUTHOR

Marcy Kennedy is a speculative fiction and suspense writer who believes fantasy is more real than you think. It helps us see life in this world in a new way and gives us a safe place to explore problems that might otherwise be too difficult to face. Alongside her own writing, Marcy works as a freelance editor and teaches classes on craft and social media through WANA International.

She's also a proud Canadian, the proud wife of a former U.S. Marine, owns five cats and a dog who weighs as much as she does, and plays board games and the flute (not at the same time). Sadly, she's also addicted to coffee and jelly beans.

You can find her blogging about writing and about the place where real life meets science fiction, fantasy, and myth at www.marcykennedy.com. To sign up for her new-release mailing list, please visit her website. Not only will you hear about new releases before anyone else, but you'll also receive exclusive discounts and freebies. Your email address will never be shared and you can unsubscribe at any time.

Contact Marcy
Email: marcykennedy@gmail.com
Website: www.marcykennedy.com
Twitter: @MarcyKennedy
Facebook: www.facebook.com/MarcyKennedyAuthor

Printed in Great Britain
by Amazon

69145158R00078